The Dream
The Glory
and
The Strife

The Dream
The Glory
and
The Strife

Editor
Raymond Fenech

First Edition

Hidden Brook Press
www.HiddenBrookPress.com
writers@HiddenBrookPress.com

Copyright © 2018 Hidden Brook Press
Copyright © 2018 Authors

All rights for poems revert to the author. All rights for book, layout and design remain with Hidden Brook Press. No part of this book may be reproduced except by a reviewer who may quote brief passages in a review. The use of any part of this publication reproduced, transmitted in any form or by any means, electronic, mechanical, photocopied, recorded or otherwise stored in a retrieval system without prior written consent of the publisher is an infringement of the copyright law.

Todos los derechos por los poemas son de los autores. Los derechos de producción del libro, montaje y diseño son de SandCrab Books. No se permite reproducir este libro, excepto por un crítico, quien podrá citar fragmentos breves. El uso de parte alguna de esta publicación ya sea reproducida, o transmitida en alguna forma o por algún medio, electrónico, mecánico, fotocopiado, grabado o almacenado o en cualquier otro formato de guardado sin consentimiento previo dado por escrito por el editor, es una violación a las leyes de derecho de autor.

The Dream The Glory and The Strife

Editor – Raymond Fenech
Cover Design – Richard M. Grove
Front Cover Image – Shane Joseph
Back Cover Image – Richard M. Grove
Layout and Design – Richard M. Grove

Typeset in Garamond
Printed and bound in Canada

The Dream The Glory and The Strife

The writers and poets speak to us
about their experiences,
some based on true events and real people
coming from various backgrounds
and walks of life,
as their sagas evolve within
each and every individual journey.

The more closely the author thinks of why he wrote, the more he comes to regard his imagination as a kind of self-generating cement which glued his facts together, and his emotions as a kind of dark and obscure designer of those facts. Reluctantly, he comes to the conclusion that to account for his book is to account for his life.

— *Richard Wright*

Table of Contents

Dear Lit Lovers – Prez Tai – *p. 1*
A Preface from our Cuba President – *p. 3*
A Foreword from our Editor – *p. 5*

List of Authors in order
as found in book

– Graham Ducker – *p. 13*
– Sterling Haynes – *p. 21*
– Bob Wood – *p. 25*
– Miguel Ángel Olivé Iglesias – *p. 29*
– Bruce Kauffman – *p. 48*
– John Hamley – *p. 52*
– John B. Lee – *p. 62*
– Manuel de Jesús Velázquez León – *p. 69*
– Jennifer Footman – *p. 75*
– Colin Morton – *p. 83*
– Chris Faiers – *p. 94*
– Miriam Estrella Vera Delgado – *p. 98*
– George Elliott Clarke – *p. 103*
– K.V. Skene – *p. 108*
– Connie Kinnell McKinney – *p. 113*
– Eugenio Ernesto González Aguilera – *p. 120*
– Debbie Carpenter – *p. 123*
– Dorothy Cox Rothwell – *p. 127*
– Hugh Hazelton – *p. 131*
– Adela González-Longoria Escalona – *p. 133*
– Heide Brown – *p. 136*
– Joanne Culley – *p. 142*

– James Deahl – *p. 146*
– Jorge Alberto Pérez Hernández – *p. 156*
– Keith Inman – *p. 169*
– Norma West Linder – *p. 174*
– James Cockcroft – *p. 183*
– Manuel García Verdecia – *p. 185*
– Lisa Makarchuk – *p. 194*
– Mary Lee Bragg – *p. 199*
– Richard Marvin Grove (Tai) – *p. 208*
– Adonay Pérez Luengo – *p. 216*
– Shane Joseph – *p. 218*
– Stella Mazur Preda – *p. 221*
– Donna Allard – *p. 225*
– Yanet Alejo Milian – *p. 232*
– Tara Kainer – *p. 233*
– Gary Rasberry – *p. 239*
– Kimberley Grove – *p. 241*
– Ernesto Galbán Peramo – *p. 250*
– Danielle Dinally – *p. 255*
– Jorge Luis Roblejo Pérez – *p. 259*
– Raymond Fenech – *p. 261*

List of Authors listed alphabetically by first name – *p. 286*
List of Photographers listed alphabetically by first name – *287*

Dear Lit Lovers:

We, the CCLA, are proud to bring you this new members' anthology, The Dream The Glory and The Strife, with international acclaimed editor, Dr. Raymond Fenech. Did you know that Raymond, Ray as we affectionately call him is Maltese. We have had international members in the past but no one from as historically interesting and exotic a place as Malta. Did you know that he is the Associate Editor of Adelaide Literary Magazine and Adelaide Publishers, based on 5th Avenue, New York and Lisbon in Portugal. The publishers have just been listed as one of the top 100 literary publications and book publishing houses in the USA. We are proud to say that he is a twice Pushcart Literary Prize nominee and was a journalist with The Times & Sunday Times of Malta. His books include, The Incident of the Mysterious Priest (short stories) and Growing with the Shadows (poetry collection) is soon to be launched at the international book fair, Expo America, New York. You can find more about him in his bio at the end of this book. I have to say that I pressured him to write a bit longer bio than the others in the book because his is our esteemed editor. Thank you Ray for doing such a fine job. You can reach him at writer@go.net.mt.

The CCLA truly is an international organization. Many times I have been asked if members have to be Canadian or Cuban. The short answer is no. We are open to members from around the world. The other linked question that I have been asked is, do I have to have ever travelled to Cuba? The equally short answer is NO! Though many of our members have travelled to Cuba and are a more rounded person for their experience but one simply has to be interested in helping to build international cultural bridges with Cuba.

Even though many of our CCLA members are politically motivated the CCLA tries hard to remain politically neutral. I have been told many times that it is impossible to be non-political and that even the very attempt of being non-political is a political statement. My argument to that is that it is our goal of not being political that is the important thing. We are not the 'Non-Political Alliance' we are a 'Literary Alliance'. The Canada Cuba Literary Alliance is proud of our cultural roots.

SO pass the word to anyone that might be interested in joining the CCLA, we truly are all international cultural bridge builders.

Prez Tai / Richard M. Grove

A Preface from our Cuba President:

Being one of the authors anthologized in this fine book, I have nothing but praise for the way the book was conceived, structured and brought to life. Only the hearts and minds of two doyens like the Anthology's seasoned Editor, Dr. Raymond Fenech, and CCLA Founding President, Richard Grove (Prez Tai), could produce such a fine piece. Thank you to both of them.

Fenech has done a fabulous job with this anthology. Not only do prose and poetry co-exist; they also overflow the pages, carved and polished with the zest of a perfectionist, as Fenech is. We are indebted to him for a job well done with the exquisite expertise he poured before, while and after he submitted his editing work to Grove. I was a sharing partner in the process, I was a grateful witness to the punctilious professionalism shown by Fenech and admired by all of us friends involved in the CCLA's quest to offer culture and friendship and high-quality books to the world.

As the CCLA Cuban President I have little if anything to add to their impressive forewords. Both have been able to condense their views on the significance that this anthology will have for readers around the world. Passion goes hand in hand with quality in this new collection. Many themes overlap and blend in harmony with each other. The authors, Cuban, Canadian and international throw themselves to the experience of living and the equally thrilling experience of putting down in words for the readers what they feel, what they fear, what they want and how they want it.

I am most grateful that the CCLA has given the Cuban authors once more, in these pages, the chance to have an international voice. Opportunities like this allow our island voice to fly beyond oceans and reach the world.

Miguel Ángel Olivé Iglesias
CCLA Cuba President

A Foreword from our Editor

The Canada Cuba Literary Alliance members' anthology has become somewhat like a beacon, the flagship of this incredible organization which embraces two nations, Cuba and Canada. They are two worlds that are so far apart when it comes to their different customs and traditions, the languages spoken and the way of life, yet strange as it may sound, the Cuban writers have become like blood brothers and sisters with their Canadian counter parts through the art of writing. I personally, as an editor, feel honoured to have been given the unique opportunity of knowing all these writers so closely, even if I'm neither a Canadian nor a Cuban, but Maltese. But who cares, literature, like sport and music has always served to breach barriers and achieve that unity which the greatest of politicians have failed to achieve throughout the centuries. There have been so many wars between countries, but never a war between artists, poets, writers and journalists?

This book is an amazing showcase of various inspirations: among others, nostalgia, love, travelling, featuring protagonists from the authors' personal memoirs, even memoirs from soldiers in WWII, nature, the environment, hurricanes, death, children, the passage of time, youth, age, death, politics, human destiny, pets, fishing, silence, the sea and various prose some based on true events and people. Reading through every submission I found this work has one thing in common, it portrays feelings, problems and various aspects and traits, which all humans who are on their short journey in this life have to put up with. In other words, the arduous task of living: surviving, struggling against all odds, falling on one's face and finding the strength to get up again: and somehow trying to smile through all the pain, grief and joy. In the end, we are all the same, one people, all waiting for God.[1]

The point is, no matter the nationality, the traditional differences, all people from any country strive towards one goal – living life to the fullest, improving its quality and surviving the human jungle, which unfortunately other abnormal, selfish and sick minded people have created with their own bare hands, affecting not only our world but also the environment.

American Poetess May Swenson says, Poetry can help man to stay human and I would add that Writing is like breathing, we cannot do without. When we finish writing something we always end up feeling elated because writing is in fact a therapy. Writers do this self-therapy and all will agree – it actually works!

Having worked for many years as a journalist and editor, I know for a fact that our writing, every single word we jot down can change something, start a ripple effect, make people cry, or laugh and even change their minds, their attitudes and their mannerisms, thus creating a better world for future generations. The Canada Cuba Literary Alliance is in fact opening its doors wider and ready to welcome all writers from any other nationality in the world.

As I have said earlier, I am Maltese, from a very small country that despite its size, was effective enough many times even to change the course of European history, especially during the siege of 1565 and WWII. Yet, in the CCLA, I feel as if I have found my home and its members have become like the greatest of friends, and at times yes, even better and more supportive than family. So, no matter where you come from, you have nothing to lose and all to gain – you can now actually experience first-hand for yourself the incredible togetherness, the unity and the support within this literary organization.

So, besides assuring readers and writers alike they will be amazed with the variety of subjects available in this anthology, they can also write to: …. for a membership application form. Everybody is a writer if he/she live in this world; because every single person has a story, or stories to tell.

Those of you who cringe at the simple mentioning of the word, 'poetry', please remember that the National Poet of Canada, Milton Acorn was considered as, The People's Poet and the reason for this was because his poems steered away from obscurity and vagueness and brought back poetry to the man on the street. After all, poetry/writing in general was originally created to entertain the masses when most people were still illiterate.

Hence why today, it's so difficult to find a professional publisher for a poetry/prose collection. Publishers want to make money. So the only way to ensure they do that is by publishing the well-known names, even if their writing is sometimes not even worth the paper it's written on. For them, it's the name that sells the book, not its contents. So to all new and aspiring writers, please be advised, the CCLA is on a mission to overturn this mentality and give poetry and writing in general back to the people.

Dr. Raymond Fenech
CCLA Ambassador, Malta

---

[1] *TV BBC series, 'Waiting for God' is a very amusing comedy about a rebellious couple living in a residential home who just don't want to give up on life just yet. Waiting for God actually means we are all expecting the end – the expiry date which each one of us are born with.*

Photograph by John Hamley

Photograph by John Hamley

Photograph by Shane Joseph

Photograph by Wency – Wenceslao Alexander Rosales

Photograph by Richard M. Grove

Graham Ducker

The Old Street Lamp

Part way down
the dead-end street
the old lamp
droops,
and sags
under the weight
of its illumination.

A cone
of melancholy
diffuses down
upon the broken sidewalk
where
an ear-flattened cat
skirts the edge.

Nothing much happens
here any more.

The lamp
remembers
itself
and new friends
standing tall,
faithfully showing
residents the way.

It recalls how,
under their watchful eyes,
children played
late into the night.

Sad memories
twist its wires
evoking
how some friends
blinked out
never to be replaced.

A couple of companions
lost their eyes
to vandalism.

The darkened neighbourhood
changed.

Gradually
families moved away,
leaving
hollow glassy eyes
to stare out over
the deserted
pavements.

A sinister atmosphere
has replaced
the community
warmth.

The old street lamp
will strive
to maintain
its protective
vigil.

Only time will tell
when it will join
its friends
in darkness.

Cuba Charisma

It is sentiment,
that changes
attitudes.

It infuses the soul.

Upon returning home
the tourist discovers
mundane chores
initiate memories
    of historic streets,
    of unseen controls,
    of enterprising people,
    of crowded markets,
    of antique cars,
    of barren shelves.

The renewed heart
appreciates:
    availability,
    convenience,
    selection,
    abundance,
    choice,
    basics.

Cuba Write up

Come. COME! Come to Cuba with me where rustling palm fronds accompanying warm waves washing white sand. Discover how your world disintegrates in a child's blazing smile. Journey to where time, space and circumstance have created a sharing – a caring society. Dare to lose your materialistic complacency in streets teeming with enterprising vendors and opportunists. Experience how the all-encompassing atmosphere slowly – decisively – suppresses your internal drive of urgency.

Come to Cuba.

I can say that now that my introduction to patience was completed upon finally settling – some ten hours later – into a neat room overlooking the Caribbean at the Motel Tropicoco.

In Cuba, time takes on a meaning of its own. The morning shuttle bus from the motel will leave more-or-less on time. The afternoon return bus, which you are supposed to meet, maybe the same bus, or a different bus; picks you up along the Malecon, or someplace nearby. For tourists used to punctual schedules, the experience can be nerve-wrecking for the first few days.

With a good map, a phrase book, and keen sense of direction and the assistance of many friendly Cubans, one will eventually settle down, relax and enjoy the flavours of Cuba.

Of course, a good reliable guide who helps you locate the right restaurants, the tourist hideaways, knows the history, will make the trip less complicated. The public washrooms are something to be experienced before the mind believes what has been forewarned. Suffices to say, keep a pack of Kleenex which must be brought handy along with numerous ten-centavo coins.

So come…COME…to a world that will forever change your worldly outlook.

Come and absorb Cuba!

Life in a Leaf

A loon's serenade drifted down the lake as the autumn sunset deepened. With toes prodding floating leaves, a Grandfather and his twelve-year-old grandson sat on the end of a dock. The cottage visit was over, so they were savouring the last moments. There wasn't much to say. It had all been said. Neither wanted to say goodbye.

The old man reached down, picked up a large maple leaf and spun it by the stem. *You know Jerry, they say a whole lifetime is written in a leaf.*

What do you mean, Grandpa?

Here, you hold it. This stem leads to the main vein. We might call it the thread of life.

The boy's finger traced the rib-line. *It's the thickest one.*

What do you notice about it as it reaches the top?

It gets thinner.

So we could say life starts out very strong, like down here and, as time passes, a person becomes more selective, more focused.

I guess people want a lot of stuff at first.

Grandpa's eyes sparkled. *Good point. Now, Grandson, what else do you notice in the leaf?*

There are lines coming from the middle one.

Yes, and just as these veins support the leaf, people grow, go to school, make friends, have families and perhaps start businesses that branch out. Many experiences shape life.

You can see all that?

The old man chuckled. *Well, as one gets older, one becomes philosophical; you think about the past.*

I suppose so", the boy nodded, *"But I don't have much of a past yet.*

That's true, but you will. The loon's call echoed the sentiments.

This leaf sure has a lot of different colours, Grandpa.

Now that you mention it, it does have all the hues you find in leaves. In fact, they could represent an entire lifetime.

Grandpa glanced at his grandson who had become quiet. *I'm sorry, Grandson, I did not mean to be a downer.*

No, no, Grandpa, I like listening to you! Tell me about the colours.

Let's do it together. Perhaps we can give them names without using 'colour' names. A wrinkled finger pointed at an area nearest the base: *What do you think of when you see this shade?*

Springtime, when the leaves first come out.

So what name can we give it without calling it light green?

How about 'New' or 'Beginning'? How about 'New Beginning'?

Sounds good to me, smiled Grandpa. *Life is just starting out. Everything is bright and fresh. Now, as we get further out, the colour becomes darker and deeper. Any ideas?*

This is the colour of summer leaves. Let's call it, 'Summer Time'.

That name fits as well as any I can think of.

Yeah, and the person is growing and learning.
The old man gently squeezed his grandson's shoulder. *You're pretty sharp.*

A self-conscious smile lit the lad's face: *Too bad the 'Summer Time' colour doesn't stay.* The boy's finger brushed the leaf. *Right here it changes to the fall shades like now.*

Have you ever heard the term: The Autumn of One's Life?

The boy nodded.

Well, what part of life could this tint represent?

Probably the time when the person is much older. Maybe he has a family, a good job, and things like that.

Right, the elderly man beamed at his grandson, *And he is probably looking forward to retiring. So, now give that shade a name.*

The boy scratched his chin. *How about 'Autumn', or 'Pumpkin', or 'Campfire' – how about 'Autumn Campfire'?*

I like it. So, now moving further out, we see our 'Autumn Campfire' changes to a red and then to brown.

A young finger ran over the leaf: *Yeah, but we can't use reddish brown. How about 'Northern Sunset'?*

Beautiful! The sunset of life! So what is the person like now?

Oh, he would be old, kinda like ... The boy stopped.

Like what?

The lad looked at his hands, and then muttered: *L ...like you, Grandpa.*

That's right! In a way, it is a great time of life. I can look back and be thankful for many things, especially for my wonderful grandson.

I suppose so.

The man continued. *So now, we are away, out here at the edge where it is dark, ragged and crumbly. Can you think of colour-name for this area?*

The leaf was flung onto the lake.

I know what it means, Grandpa, and I am not naming that colour!

Silence descended as toes prodded leaves. A youthful hand slid across and tightly took hold of the wrinkled one. *I don't want you to die, Grandpa.*

The old man squeezed the boy's hand. *Thank you, Grandson. I have to stick around to*

watch you grow up, don't I?

A loon's moan drifts down the lake.

How about we go in for a hot chocolate?

I'd like that!

About the author

Graham Ducker's memoir book: Don't Wake the Teacher; is an integral part of Holguin University Teachers' College. He has also published a book of poetry: Observations of Heart and Mind and won the 2006 Lichen Arts Contest. In April 2008, he delivered a key-note address at the International WEFLA Education Conference in Cuba. Email: jgrahamd@rogers.com]

Sterling Haynes

Alarming

Beep – Beep – Beep – Beep
I am becoming an alarmist?
On my 88th – it just snuck up on me,
my gawd, it wasn't intentional!
My house is wired for sound, that
sometimes goes *Beep* in the night.
It wakes a deaf octogenarian,
who can't find his glasses.

I pondered many questions:
is the sound inside or out;
a truck backing up; a burglar alarm
on my car; or the in-my-house beeper?
My wake up alarm clock or
the smoke alarm, perhaps change the
batteries? The carbon monoxide
detectors scream, my dog howls.
Call the gas company, evacuate
the house and neighbors too!

I have all the alert devices,
on the wall, on my wrist or a necklace
should I fall, stroke out or stop
breathing. I am over-prepared for
life's catastrophes. False alarms give
me panic attacks which promote
flight or fight, a call to arms – *alarme'*.
I have never cried wolf, where is the
the danger? I am an alarmist now!

Where is that damn sound coming from?
My computer, furnace, or hot water heater?
B-Be-Bee-Beep-Beep.....

Dr. Miyazaki – Enemy Alien

We interrupt this musical program to bring you a special news bulletin. This morning, December 7th, 1941, the Japanese have attacked Pearl Harbour, Hawaii, by air.

With this news, the smoldering resentment against the Japanese was brought to the boiling point. Racism turned to violence in Vancouver, British Columbia. With the fall of Hong Kong and the loss or capture of 2,000 Canadian soldiers on December 25, 1941 revenge, racism towards the Japs was rampant. The police and the army believed that the many Japanese people who lived along the Pacific coast were no threat to Canada.

Prime Minister Mackenzie King and his cabinet thought otherwise and they set up a protected area, an area extending 100 miles inland from the Pacific Ocean. All Japanese men, women and children living within these boundaries were declared enemy aliens and were then transported to the detention centre in the animal stables, at Hastings Park in Vancouver. From there, they were relocated to prison war camps in Shantytowns in the Kootenays and the interior to such places, as Greenwood, Kaslo and Lillooet/Bridge River.

Among the enemy aliens sent to Lillooet/Bridge River camp was Dr. Miyazaki and his wife, Sumiko. The doctor had been born in Yokahama, but had come to Vancouver, at age 14 in 1913 to join his father. He was a good student and soon learned English. He graduated from University of BC with a BA, but could not complete his medical degree in Canada, being Japanese. By working as a waiter, he put himself through medical training and he graduated from the Kirkville School of Osteopathy in Missouri. On May 15, 1930 he was licensed by the BC College of Physicians and Surgeons. He had a successful medical practice in Vancouver until December 7th, 1941. The next day, he and his wife were sent to stables in Hasting Park. In the spring, they were moved to Bridge River's Taylor enclosure, a primitive POW camp.

In 1944, the local doctor, Dr. Patterson, died in Lillooet. There was no doctor, coroner, midwife, police doctor, dentist or veterinarian within 100 miles. The police, mayor and council moved the good doctor and family to Lillooet and reclassified them from being: *Enemy aliens to foreign aliens*.

Dr. Miyazaki was allowed to buy a new Plymouth car and given food stamps and gasoline rations and in return, he was asked to provide medical services to the citizens of Lillooet, Bridge River/ Bralorne, all the people living along the Pacific Great Eastern [P.G.E.] railway line and all the whistle stops in between. He was also appointed coroner and police doctor.

The inventive doctor devised special chains for his car in order to travel the snowy passes and muddy roads. He had metal bars and horse shoe nails welded onto the tire chains to allow him to travel in all seasons. Initially, he travelled the rails on a speeder and later modified the speeder into a closed-in ambulance to carry at PGE worker, a stretcher and a doctor and equipment. This rail road ambulance was popular with the local doctors for years during blizzards, avalanches and mud slides. In 1946, the town of Lillooet purchased an ambulance. The good doctor made the initial down payment of $200.00 and was asked by the mayor to store the vehicle in his personal garage.

He was busy doing home deliveries, pulling teeth and doing house calls long distances. At one time, he made a house call on the Niskip Indian Reserve. The woman had a uterine hemorrhage and in the middle of winter with his car chains attached, he managed to climb the terrifying Texas Creek Hill and do D&C [Dilatation and Curettage] in her bedroom with sterile curettes. Another time, he attended a young boy who, while riding a sled, was scalped by the undersurface of a car in the village of Pavillion. In the general store, he reattached the scalp using the store's counter top as an operating table. He supplied his special portable operating room lights during the procedure.

In Lillooet, he ran a clinic from his house where he housed sick patients in his upstairs. New mothers and newborns were his main patients. He pulled teeth, ran a weekly VD clinic, held a veterinarian clinic, was the local meteorologist and took police pictures when acting as provincial coroner. In the heat of summer, he became a reluctant embalmer/undertaker.

For recreation, he was involved with the Boy Scout movement with his son, and organized jamborees. Dr. Mas was the first Canadian – Japanese elected alderman, he served Lillooet for five years. He organized the first Stampede in July, 1945 and was usually an appointed judge in the Indian Pretty Baby Contest during the festivities. He was active in the BPO Elks of Canada and elected Freeman of the Village in 1970.

Sadly he was transferred to Kamloops' Royal Inland Hospital in renal failure and diabetes and spent two years on dialysis. He returned to his beloved Lillooet in 1972 and was elected president of their historical society in 1973. He wrote a fascinating book called, *My Sixty Years in Canada*, which was self-published in 1973.

Dr. Miyazaki and editor Ma Murray of the Lillooet /Bridge River News both received the Order of Canada in 1977.

The good doctor died in 1984 and willed his house to the town of Lillooet. This historical house is open to the public and features his library, offices and medical equipment and is managed by the town's historical society. The doctor was innovative, compassionate and dedicated: he was a good guy. I know editor Ma Murray would echo my words with: *And that's fer damshure.*

Previously published by Rogers Publishing

About Author

Sterling Haynes is a retired MD and has published widely in newspapers, journals, anthologies and magazines. He has published many poems and written three books of stories: the first called "Bloody Practice" was a B.C. Best seller. A few years ago he won the Okanagan Arts Councils award for literary accomplishments. In his 90th year, Sterling is working on his 4th book and continues to write as a freelancer. Email: jshaynes@shaw.ca

Bob Wood

The Budget

On a long ago budget day, a procedural quirk
put a simple regional ward councillor
in a position to freeze the police budget.
Ward councillors don't obstruct police budgets
because as we all learned as kids,
the police(man) is our friend,
does important and dangerous work
protects and keeps us safe and
for all of this deserves to be well paid.

These are things that ward councillors,
even simple ones, should understand.
But since the common sense drumbeat
set the revolution in motion,
we have come to know that the best government is
to have practically no government at all
and respect for hard earned taxpayer's dollars
is the order of the day.
Others are compelled to run their ship tightly,
while the law and order liner sails unimpeded
through the calm waters of political indifference.

On that budget day, the simple ward councillor
having for a time, ascended
to the lofty heights of budget committee member,
advanced what was (by his own humble admission)
a particularly persuasive presentation
convincing the one colleague who needed convincing
that police spending should be apprehended and
it was a great day for local democracy,
or at least it seemed that way.
But the votes aren't counted
until the politicians raise their hands
and when they did
the police got their money, as they always do.

No media or public witnessed the sad event though
police brass made time in otherwise busy days
to behold the councillor's misbegotten manoeuvre.
Following his 15 minutes of small town fame
our councillor drove his car like an undertaker.
Even now, my lane changes are by-the-book perfect
and inviolable police budgets escalate still.

The author took the following material from the Regimental Diaries of the Sherbrooke Fusiliers also known as the 27th Armoured Regiment of the Canadian Army.

Lt. Colonel M.B.K. Gordon, the Regimental Commander, was the author of the Regimental Diaries. Bob's father shared some stories with him, but never wrote anything about his experiences so the author filled in some blanks with the help of his service record which he received from the Department of National Defence.

His father, S.W. (Bill) Wood, was a Lieutenant in the Sherbrooke Fusiliers when we was wounded in France and reported as dangerously ill on August 25, 1944. He recovered and was later promoted to Captain. He died in 2006 at the age of 86.

Captain Bill Wood was recipient of the 1939-45 Star, the France and Germany Star, the Defence Medal, and the Canadian Volunteer Service Medal and Clasp. He was mentioned in dispatches for distinguished service.

Found in the War Diary of the Sherbrooke Fusiliers
These extracts were written by the author's father ....

June 4-6 1944

High winds and low clouds stall D-Day 24 hours.
In spite of the wind the flotilla sails southward
all night via charted channel waters. Men ruminate
over what awaits on shore then land is sighted
at 1000 hrs off Berniere-Sur-Mere. Craft start
the run in to the beach, men quite calm
sitting on top of their vehicles watch the shore.
The Regiment lands, moves forward, no casualties
but next day German tanks make a first appearance,
force the CDN infantry to retire with 63 killed,
wounded or missing. Later, ready to move on
a half hour notice, the sun sets amidst black
banks of clouds leaving a dirty red smudgy sky
with the boom of distant gunfire broken
by the sharper rattle of nearby machine guns.
Everything seems ominous. Everyone is on alert.

July 18, 1944

The shadow of death passes over Headquarters.
In minutes, 21 cm mortars take thirty-one lives.
Heavier casualties than a normal day's fighting.

August 25, 1944

An extensive map issue arrives showing vast distances and fabulous advances imagined by HQ. Startling indeed, as those left from D-Day recall the slow, difficult struggle for CAEN and the devastating exploitation and FALAISE assault. Two days later considerable friction develops among all command levels. Little is accomplished due to the lack of appreciation by the Infantry of issues arising using armour in country where dense woods greatly limit the traversing of guns.

September 1944 – May 1945

A few men who were through the thickest fighting are a little jittery yet but doing well and should soon be over it as the Regiment fights on in NWE.

About the Author

Bob Wood has been a manager and front-line worker in the non-profit sector for many years. Over the last twenty years he has been a freelance writer and social media contributor for many publications. His focus has been on politics, sports, and social justice. Bob is a recovering municipal politician. His father served with the Sherbrooke Fusiliers in Northwest Europe returning to Canada in 1946. Email: timberline24@hotmail.com

Miguel Ángel Olivé Iglesias

Ocean Painting
"And my sea once more" Pablo Neruda

Tonight the sea is a perfumed canvas
I dare fill with hues of green
and blue and white and red;
inside my brain
the humid sounds
of the waves fondle me
as they unify with wind and rain
and hasten to the shore
in a ceaseless clash
of water and earth,
sprinkling the anchored boats
swaying them rhythmically.

Above, a dying moon competes with me
applies dabs across the canvas
light brushes, shushes
its strokes of sleepy sunlight
with her silvery touches
leaving an omen of peace.

The ocean explodes beneath the clouds
in shades of colors,
carved ripples
curved crests of foam,
and whispering tongues
echoing its vanity
praising its own greatness.

My Ocean
"Swimming towards you" Katharine Beeman

Under the greeting sun
I squint my eyes,
powerful rivers with colorful visions
illuminate me;
it is my peaceful ocean:
clouds above are mirrored
in the majestic
waltzing waves
rolling relentlessly, repeatedly
towards the coastline,
ending in an embrace
of sand and fizzing foam.

I open my eyes,
my sea bustles freshened by drizzling rain
teeming depths of green, blue and red
contours of impeccable white sails,
ghost galleons adrift in the dashing wind,
long lost forgotten tales
of swashbuckling pirates,
fearless weather-beaten men;
images of boats dotted
by God's paintbrush on a seascape.

Seated before its immensity
the enchanting sea-scent floats
to enfold me in its loving arms
lifts me and carries me
into the strong embrace
with my ocean …

Muse

Out there an ocean of boats rumbles
as you pose before my eyes,
the welcome rains align
to show me the universe in the atlas of your body.

I coin words as you model;
with you come green, blue tides
that advance and recoil with the wind
and are set free to roll under the clouded sun.

Each metaphor carries a sprinkle of flawless white,
sugar and salt
to balance the measure of desire;
but they overflow,
they become perfumed hurricanes, love poems
as you parade before me
like a Goddess of the sea,
the peace that tempts me to write

worshipping and missing you,
each time you turn to leave;
the tides subside into a slumber –
until you return to me.

Love Affair

The blue ocean dwells within me
it vibrates in languages of boats, sand, reefs, winds
crashing waves, salt, red sun, tides
endless flows that never tire,
never cease to intrigue me
when speaking about awesome tempests
under the dying light.

The sea is my endless love affair
it rolls and rumbles under the clouds
a river surfing in my eyes, in my brain
sneaking into my favourite list of aromas
soaking my feet
gently washing away my strenuous days of trepidation
my rough nights of sleeplessness.

I go back home
I must say good-bye to it – until I find another
reason to return –
but I go home *healed*
carrying the sun on my cheeks
the taste of salt in my mouth,
and warm white sand
that refuses to leave
my gratified skin.

Previously published in The Ambassador. Volume 014,
ISSN 1170 7954, September 2017 by the
Canada Cuba Literary Alliance.

Language
"Water speaks to me" Louise Halfe

The depths of the ocean
murmur in the night as I venture out in my boat.
I can't see it, just hear its rumble
fondling my ears.

Saline phrases
lapping, rebounding
recoiling and frolicking in rain and wind,
spiraling in endless motion under the clouds;
sometimes roughly, sometimes gently,
inundating towards the sleepy shore
inscribing the white sand with green foamy hieroglyphs
and blue pelagic signs.

The sea tells me
mermaid legends,
tragic whale sagas of red-blood tainted waters
tales of storms, sweeping gales,
struggle, loss, consternation
victory, hope, love.

For a few seconds it seems there's peace:
it holds its coral reef tongue
just flows, gushes, spills
leaps, springs, frisks
then again the rumbling, it caresses
it is one with its brother
who understands – the fortune of the chosen –
the powerful language
of its Triton soul.

Highway to Hell

The Arizona sky bent quietly above the torrid desert like an immense ocean of clear spaces, cloudy patches under a scorching sun. The highway was a thin, silvery streak and was solitary, except for a wide-load truck rocketing along the dusty, bumpy road. Ryan was in a hurry. The Company had already filed serious complaints about him, so his omission from the yearly share was about to become a reality.

This particular *cargo* was to be delivered A.S.A.P. This meant Ryan needed to impress his Company bosses and consequently, keeping his job. Obviously, he was in a hurry – but the road was not an easy one. Sweat trickled abundantly down his distressed face as he saw the sun slowly dipping westwards. He was still in good time but he hated driving at night along bumpy roads. The truck's engine roared steadily – Ryan pressed the pedal to the limit and the truck shot forward into the fast approaching dusk. He laid back on his seat. This would be the last trip, *Yeah*. Earning money driving across unknown areas was not Ryan's favorite cup of tea really. He had taken the long-forgotten shortcut which meant he would be facing unexpected ruts ahead of him but – It was necessary, absolutely necessary ... time was not in his favour

Unfortunately, Ryan was anticipating the troubles he would be having through the old road. Far ahead, a sharp corner/bend of the road was awaiting him. Cars had to pass a narrow stretch, protected by frangible-looking fences that overlooked a precipice. It was the roughest leg of the trip. Hundreds of feet below, a canyon –and Ryan was afraid of heights. But he had to make it! Money and job were at stake! He tried to cast away these ugly thoughts from his mind. The night, instead of bringing fear, would be his best ally in crossing the path. That was it! He would not see the cliff below! Encouraged by that self-reassuring notion, he pressed the accelerator. The truck cut through the night wind like a knife and charged ferociously towards the area. The starry sky, clear and cloudless now, was signaling that he would make it and deliver the merchandise on time. He was already seeing all that Cash, green dollar bills filling his hands! The possibility of retaining his job was enticing in his mind.

Suddenly, the truck's engine made a funny noise and stopped. Ryan panicked and looked at the dashboard, the needles on the counters were dead. He cursed and pulled over with the help of the friction left. The massive trailer rolled slowly off the road, over the sandy patch before coming to a halt. Ryan cursed once more. No big deal! An experienced trucker like him could fix whatever was wrong with the engine in a jiffy! He tried the ignition twice; the engine merely pinged. Losing his temper, Ryan pressed the clutch repeatedly and tried the ignition time and again, until the powerful thing growled back to life. Lucky break! Ryan steered to the left and re-entered the road speeding up to recover the wasted minutes.

The dangerous corner of the road was in sight. Ryan felt weak but struggled to keep focused. The night would be his friend, surely! He slowed down and faced the cliff. The ascent was painful. He had to constantly gear to first then shift to second for a stronger pull, until the truck was way high up on the cliff. The first part of the narrow road had already been left behind. But the harrowing drive down through the narrow stretch was still a fearsome thought on his mind. He had to do it! He gripped the steering-wheel and drove on with ease. He couldn't see anything on the passenger side, and his mind began to play tricks on him. Fear was building and images of his trailer falling off the edge flashed through his head. He switched to low-beam and half-closed his eyes, trying his best to eliminate all negative thoughts. Endless seconds passed by, the endless narrow stretch was little by little overcome. When Ryan found himself well away from the area, he heaved a sigh of relief and put on the brakes. He had made it! Now all that was left was to get there at full speed, deliver the stuff and return by train. With a fat pay cheque of course!

Ryan was contemplating the distant horizon, smiling, almost laughing, when a drop of water landed on his windshield: *What the hell?*

He looked up and realized that the sky had turned cloudy and the stars had vanished. It looked heavy, full of untimely, and unwelcome rain. Ryan cursed, for the third time. He did hate night driving, bumpy roads, cliffs and damn rain! And he was in a hurry. Now the road had become slippery with the rain that had accumulated huge amounts of desert sand, mixed with dirt. Ryan turned the high-beam on. The wipers were useless to prevent the cold rain from steaming the sun-fried glass screen and Ryan had to work hard to drive and keep his eyes on the right lane. He had been lucky that no other car had ventured into the corner. The truck's lights would have surely blinded any driver ... Abruptly, miraculously, the rain stopped. Now the town was closer! Ryan's mind harbored sweet hopes, his throat produced a high-spirited sound when a dazzling billboard greeted his already bloodshot eyes. WELCOME! *Great!* He would make it before dawn and would be back home to find shelter in his wife's arms.

Actually, Linda had been upset that he would have to travel all night across that *highway to hell*, as she had described it. But he was sure that once back home, she would forget the whole affair and would not walk out on him: *Money to dine and wine, so everything's fine*, thought Ryan, and smiled wickedly. The road was dry again and Ryan let the truck easily swallow up the miles left ... YOU ARE NOW ENTERING ... The billboard caressed Ryan. He felt drowsy but elated.

Only two and a half miles to the destination where some folks would pick up the merchandise and pay him. *Cash! Nice word, yeah!* Ryan took a look at his watch. It was three thirty-two a.m. In less than five minutes, the deal would be settled. *Yeah.* He had had to throw himself away and run the risk of transporting the *merchandise* with the legal façade of a Highway Transport Company. Well, there had been no way out of this. Not doing this one little favor to his bosses meant he wouldn't get any money.

Ryan drove into the sleepy town and approached the meeting spot. His heart was pounding and all traces of drowsiness had vanished. He located the small garage, drove to it and stopped the truck. *Where the hell are those guys?* For a moment, he felt a tinge of concern and butterflies in his stomach. He waited a few seconds, got back on the truck and turned its lights on and off. That was the signal.

Two men came out of the garage holding a black case each. Ryan waited until they were near, then opened the door and jumped out onto the street. *Did you bring the stuff?* The man talking to Ryan took a step forward.

Yeah. Come and check. The same man walked to the back of the truck with Ryan, who unlocked the big doors. The man leaped into the truck and saw closed boxes that he ignored. Instead, he raised one hand and operated with swift dexterity a simulated knob in the truck's top panel. It silently slid backwards and left revealed small packs neatly stacked and attached to the top.

It's OK, Dan! Give this man what's his, he said, closing up the panel.

The man on the street smiled and handed Ryan a black case. Ryan's face brightened as he opened the case and his eyes saw brand-new bills orderly placed inside the case. Two million bucks! Enough to start leading a decent life. To hell with the job and the problems! Ryan smiled, childishly, and lifted his eyes. Suddenly his smile turned quickly into a grimace. His eyes opened wide and the case handle slipped from his fingers and fell from his hands still unclosed.

Dan was standing before him with a sneer on his face and a gun firmly held in his hand pointed at Ryan: *What…what the hell is this*, shouted Ryan?

Just that, answered the man, *Hell, just that*, as he repeatedly shot Ryan dead.

Thou Shalt Honour Thy Father

We take people for granted and fail to see the beauty and meaning they naturally bring into our daily lives. It was only when my sister called me to let me know my father was very ill, I started to realize I had taken him for granted. But, I was working miles away from home and the call came in, late at night. I waited for daybreak to start my journey home. That night was a harrowing experience of anguish and revelation as the hours ticked slowly away. It was then that the first flashbacks of my childhood memories flooded me ...

My father was kind and loving, yet very strict with my misbehavior or encroachments. He never missed a single occasion to please my mother with poetry reading sessions and serenades, followed by bowls of chocolate candies from which my sister and I always received our generous share. He was *the best Daddy there is*, as most children would call theirs and would be proud to show off to their classmates...

But, at thirteen, I sort of changed, distancing myself away from a father who was always busy but just the same had found the time to take me with him on his journeys and in his way incept in my mind – scraps of knowledge. I was an introvert. Even after these many years, I have not been able to clearly figure out the reasons. I blame it on my edgy temperament and the long seasons that I was spending away from home. All I know is that it was there, like a wall of bricks I had laid between the two of us, and seemed to be there even when I definitely moved on to another town.

That's when my sister phoned me. I took it calmly at first, and was almost incredulous hoping, it was not my father she was talking about. Crude reality hit me below the belt: there was *my* father – *the best Daddy there is* – hooked up to plastic tubes, attached to a lie-supporting machine cooped up in a gloomy hospital room. The vision of vitality I had always had of my father was brutally collapsing before my eyes. The man in front of me was an old man, engulfed by a death-like aura as white as a sheet

...

Days and nights slipped away as we took care of him. Now, I confess, in those hours came the revitalization of our relationship. The son learned to show and administer affection and attention to his father. The son saw his father's return to life and to his heart. He recovered with the months, after he underwent two life-risking operations.

I still cherish those days at the hospital, when I took him for slow-paced walks. He would confidently place his hand upon my shoulder and I would gently hold him around the waist. Never had I been so emotionally attached to my father. Doctors, nurses, orderlies, patients would pause and smile at such a harmonious father-son relationship. Father and son embraced, conquering inches, conquering life, conquering each other.

Yes, I had taken my father for granted. I had forgotten that having him there at my disposal was not everything, when I ought to have patted him on the back and told him, *Hey, Dad, I love you*, and try to get the most out of our lives together. We needed that, **I** needed that. I had let years go by before life struck me like lightning making me realize, living means also sharing and lovingly others openly and giving our all and receiving the same devotion.

Today, I feel redeeming warmth coming from those moments when my father and I became entirely interrelated beings after I had been a blind, haughty adolescent for so long. I am grateful he is here now to share my life with him. And to honor him, even when death do us a part.

Perfection

A flicker of light filtered into Arnold´s room. It was dark and silent. The dim luminescence fell upon the body of a woman, revealing her impeccable beauty, striving to scout her height. She was simply one of a kind; an utterly well-built woman. The black waves of her vast crop of hair cascaded down over her back, almost touching the threshold of her hips. The arc of her eyebrows had a perfect shape, matching the depth of her eyes, night-black and piercing. Her nose was in synchronization with her sensuous frame of her lips, and the smooth contours of her face ended in a sharp-pointed chin.

Her full height was visible. Her neck was slender and soft, set on shoulders sculptured with the magical complement of her long arms. Her body matched the perfection of her beauty; an outlined flawless design. No scars, no stains, simply faultless. Her back was slightly arched, endowing her with a grandiose posture never seen before. Her sexy legs, long and smooth, enhanced her unique poise.

A front view revealed breasts that reminded one of the crescents of the moon, with a splendid abdomen. She was slim, like a ballerina but her hips heavenly wide. There was really nothing to take away, nothing to add. Nothing was spared to create such a sculptured female model, producing the very ultimate of a sublime being; what was not used was not needed at all. Perhaps, something could mar – or enhance her design, but this was a simple matter of personal taste – a tiny mole on the left end of her lip, a beauty spot. This actually proved to be more enhancing to her picturesque face.

Her figure was complemented by a set of very delicate feet that seemed to touch the floor so lightly that when she walked, she seemed to float on air. Under that glimmer of light, she looked even more ravishing, mysterious, as she was caught in the shadows of the moment ...

The sound of a key turning in the door lock cracked the crypt-like silence. She did not move. Slowly, the door opened and the silhouetted figure of a tall man walked into the room. It was Arnold. The woman remained still and silent. He closed the door behind him, and switched on the lamp. The light seemed almost harmful to the eyes, to the magical mystery and beauty which lay before him. Slowly, he started to strip off his clothes. Then, slowly he moved towards her, until he came face to face with the woman. He slipped both hands around her naked waist. Then gently and slowly he started caressing her body curves, whilst whispering sweet nothings in her ears.

He stopped for a moment. Then spoke for the first time, in his tenor voice that broke the silence in the room with its melodious gentle tone: *This time the prize will be mine, he smiled, No other human contestant will ever build as perfect an android as this I have in front of me …*

About the Author

Miguel Ángel Olivé Iglesias is the Canada Cuba Literary Alliance president in Cuba, member of the Mexican Association of Language, and Literature Professors and vice-president of the Shakespeare Studies Centre. Master and Associate Professor at Holguín University, his poetry touches upon people, life, family and nature. He uses poems in class, on-campus and in community activities, adding a formative element to his production. Email: migueloi@femsu.uho.edu.cu

Photograph by John Hamley

Photograph by Shane Joseph

Photograph by John Hamley

Photograph by Wency – Wenceslao Alexander Rosales

Photograph by John Hamley

Photograph by John Hamley

Bruce Kauffman

absolutely

to absolutely
know the all
of the next
      things coming

but in each
      instant
as each new
thing arrives
      incredulous
      still
it's in its own
      beauty
in its own
      fresh
      newness

each instant
as old
      as the all
      of time
and equally
as new and
as full
      of itself
as the very
first breath
of any
thing
      newborn

A Movie, and More, Started it All

I was writing in a small, quiet café early this morning and as I put down my pen to enjoy both the silence and my coffee, I realized that sometimes it takes decades, even a lifetime, to see how just one small detail in front of me now, began as something else. Anything today in my life may have looked completely different then – seemingly separate, isolated, alone. But that every single detail is always, like a sprouting seed growing into something larger, expanding over time. It is the ever-flowing evolution of only seemingly mismatched and isolated *things* coming together. And I wond-ered if I am often only able to see, how it all evolves and connects reflectively, as I look back on it with a wiser outlook.

Then a single thought took me back in time. First, I must admit that I am not a big fan of the idea of any *anniversary*. Those days and dates in *time* seem little more than artificial on our small, static calendars when compared to the *All* of *Real Time*. After all, even Einstein posited: *Time is an illusion*. But these hypotheses are for me, perhaps, a subject better left to another writer with a bolder pen.

My resistance, though, to honouring anniversary dates faltered a bit this morning. It seems there was one exception – poetry. The importance and significance of what poetry writing meant to me all these years. I realized this morning, I have been writing poetry for 50 years this month. And the thought of it occurred to me not as a loud exclamation of accomplishment. Not at all. Instead, the thought crossed my mind as a soft and gentle whisper: that I'd been lucky to want to put into words those things I felt and sensed. I was humbled, in the presence of all other writers, authors, poets, and artists around me.

And not fifty years, but two decades ago, I started to become *obsessed* with poetry. It became and continued to be the foundation upon which I could define myself. It was that constant, single life-force, other than just my heartbeat and breath, which gave me the drive to go through each and every new day. I believe it was, and still is that vital for me.

This morning, though, as I began to take a more focused look back down that long poetry-filled road, I wanted to discover the *seed* of it – to embrace it. To honour it.

It was not to be found in a book, or even a written text, but instead in a movie, *Doctor Zhivago*. I'd seen it as an impressionable teen, fifteen years old in the late 1965/66. I connected to it immediately, in the first scene of his mother's death and then in the barrenness and beauty of the landscape, the cinematography, that followed it. And of course, the full story. I was mesmerized as I sat that night watching the movie and wanted to be Yuri Zhivago. And not Yuri Zhivago the doctor, but the poet, the man.

I don't believe that this *seed* to write poetry immediately sprouted in me then, but my love for the movie lingers still and sends a wonderful shiver up my spine, even at the thought of it. I have watched the movie dozens of times since, but still in each, remember sitting there the first time and wishing I was a poet.

I realize, now this morning, the movie simply sowed that *seed* of becoming a poet inside me. And my heart and mind were then not yet prepared, or fertile enough to germinate. That happened two years later, when in my Grade 12 English class, the teacher brought to our attention several less traditional poets and their works. That allowed me to see the full scenario of what poetry was all about. We, in that class that day, were then given the task of writing a poem within fifteen minutes. I don't remember the poem I wrote, but I do remember that even though I was at first reticent about the idea of having to write one, once I started, I very much enjoyed the process and how it felt. And later that fall, and in my first few days at university, I wrote my second poem – the one I remember and still have.

It's really funny how fifty years can pass so quickly. But you don't realize until you look back. Maybe I misjudged the importance of anniversaries, and history. Of how we try to put things in place that way. To recognize, quantify, justify, but also to honour and to embrace them.

And as I do that this morning, I realize that with this movie, I need to confess that perhaps this *seed* grew together with another planted many years earlier. Perhaps those two seeds merged, as a hybrid of some sort. That even earlier the *seed* comes to me now as a beautiful soft memory of my mother, often reading and sometimes reciting a particular poem to us just before bed, *Wynken, Blynken, and Nod* (Eugene Field, 1889). I remember as well, on some nights as we were tucked into bed, she was set to read something else and I asked if she could read that instead.

Again, all of this is in no way intended for me to feel like I've accomplished something in my years of poetry, or even my life. Far from it. No, it is for me just a soft and gentle reminder of how long I've been here. Of how deeply my life has been touched and enriched by other poets, and authors – and even a movie. Humbled by the greatness of it all, I feel I must now honour all of that, and all of them. And whilst upon this morning's journey down memory lane, I realize that long before the movie I credit for my talent, it was first my mother's soft voice long ago – and the way we were mesmerized and warmed by the gentle sound of it in our beds as we peacefully nodded off to sleep.

About the Author

Bruce Kauffman, a poet, writer, editor, and a spoken word radio show programmer and host, lives in Kingston, ON, Canada. His work has appeared in a number of journals and anthologies, and has had two chapbooks and three full collections published. Email: bruce.kauffman@hotmail.com

John Hamley

3 Haiku

A woodcock nests
beak-deep in snow
little black eye on me

> *"A woodcock nests"*
> *previously published in*
> *World Haiku Review.*

A grouse drums
so close
the house drums

The queen of butterflies
her name pinned
in Latin

Little Encounter

In Holguín, the old streets are narrow and so are their sidewalks, often only wide enough for one person on one side, and for two to walk side by side on the other. And that is not enough. Front steps of houses protrude onto the sidewalks. Lamp posts and other posts are—guess where – on the sidewalk. Often, you have no choice but to step into the traffic to get around them.

Yet some major arteries run on narrow one-way streets. Traffic flows, sometimes fast, sometimes slow, cars, trucks, motorcycles with side cars, buses, bicycles, horse carts, pedestrians mingle, horns honk, people pop in and out of the houses, vendors get in everybody's way, children play on the sidewalk – where else? It is a zoo, but miraculously no one ever seems to get hurt.

When the evening falls, traffic on side streets thins down to a trickle and the street turns into an extension of the living rooms. After all, it is only an open door and two or three steps down. Neighbors see neighbors, chat on the sidewalk, children run hither and thither, socialize, play ball. Men bring out tables to under streetlights to play dominos. Most nights, a group of young men sets up a big table near my house and plays table tennis on it.

One evening, I stopped to take pictures of them. There was barely enough light, so I stayed for quite a while, trying to catch the players between strokes so that the pictures wouldn't blur. An old woman came by and said something to me, and I told her that I didn't understand and that I was a Canadian. We talked for a few minutes within the limits of my vocabulary, and when she began to move on, I took her by the shoulders and kissed her on the cheek. She kissed me back and walked away.

The Virgin of Cobre

Over four hundred years ago, three men, two Indians and a Black slave, all named Juan, went in a small boat to the Nipe Bay, off the Atlantic coast to collect salt for the slaughterhouse at Barajagua, which supplied meat for the copper mining community of El Cobre near the present-day city of Santiago de Cuba. Their boat was caught by a storm. They prayed to the Virgin Mary for protection and when the skies cleared and the storm was gone, there was a small wooden statue of Virgin Mary floating on the waves. She was holding baby Jesus in one arm and a golden cross on the other. Her clothes, which were made of real cloth, were still dry.

Many years later one of the men, the slave Juan Moreno, testified that the statue had been on top of a small wooden plank which bore the inscription *Yo Soy la Virgen de la Caridad, I am the Virgin of Charity*.

When the men returned to Barajagua, they took the statue with them, and a small chapel was built for her there. But there are several versions of this story – she kept disappearing from there even when the doors were locked, and then reappearing somewhere else. The third time, she was found by a young girl picking flowers and chasing butterflies on a small hill, overlooking El Cobre. People decided that that was where she wanted to be, and built a church for her on that spot.

Many miracles have been attributed to her. On one wall of the church, there is a large collection of crutches and other walking aid devices that people who no longer needed them, have left there as a token of their suffering. She has become Cuba's national saint, loved and revered by almost all Cubans, regardless of their religious beliefs, or political orientation.

Many pilgrims come to El Cobre to light candles and pray to the Virgin Mary in her church. Many of them bring sunflower coronas, larger than dinner plates, or bundles of other flowers to lay on her altar. You can see vendors of such flowers along the highways, long before you come to El Cobre, and in El Cobre itself, you will see them lining both sides of the road, stepping out as far onto the pavement as they dare, trying to sell their coronas to every car that approaches the church.

Once, I asked a Catholic friend: how can a wooden statue become a saint? She told me: *They are all the Virgin Mary. She appears in different guises.*

At the end of March 2012, Pope Benedict XVI came to visit Cuba to meet with President Raúl Castro and to pay his respects to the Virgin Mary on the 400th Anniversary of her discovery. This was a big event for Cuba, and in honor of it the Government of Cuba declared a civic holiday for Good Friday. Not a Church holiday, as Cuba maintains a separation between religion and the State, but a holiday anyhow, for people to celebrate in whichever way they wanted.

One evening, about two weeks before the Pope's arrival, I was visiting Manuel. He was watching the eight o'clock news, as he usually does after dinner. All of a sudden, he stiffened up in his chair and said to me: *Something very important is happening right now. Something that has never happened before. A group of people have occupied a church. They are refusing to leave. They say that they have a message for the Pope.*

At first, the Church asked the Government to leave the protesters alone, but later, as they interfered with people who came there to worship, changed its mind and asked the police to remove the protesters, but not to bring any weapons inside the church. Next day, somebody told me that a single unarmed officer had walked into the church and persuaded the protesters to leave, with a promise that there would be no reprisals against them.

Had I known, I could have witnessed that kind of a thing happening right there in Holguín. The day before the Pope arrived, a group of protesters entered the big cathedral beside Flowers' Park and refused to leave. When the evening came, the priest told them that he had to close the doors for the night, so now they really had to go. But they still refused, so the priest called the police. The police sent six or seven particularly tall and broad-shouldered officers to discuss the matter with the protesters, and the protesters left without further incident.

The Pope's visit passed happily, almost without a hitch. But not quite. According to the BBC News, shortly before the Pope celebrated the mass in front of a crowd of about 200,000 people in Santiago de Cuba, one man shouted: *Down with Communism!* Others in the audience booed him and shouted: *Cuba, Cuba, Cuba!* The man was taken then away by the police.

Much later, after I had returned to Canada and was scanning the internet for some information on Cuba, I happened to land on the web site of some political dissidents in Holguín. They were complaining they had been ordered to stay in the city until the Pope had left the country, and that one of them had tried to leave, but was turned back by the police at the bus station.

Lookout Hill

One day Miriam, Adonay, Manuel, Pablo, Tony and I drove to the top of a lookout hill with the car to take pictures. No sooner were we out of the car, then an attractive young woman greeted us, offering to sell us necklaces. But I had already bought all the necklaces I wanted, so I politely declined her.

In that case, she responded with a smile, *I will give you this one for free,* and handed me a pretty little bracelet of red and brown beads. I accepted it, also with a smile, and put it in my pocket. And then …from nowhere, like a vulture, an old woman descended on us and asked me for a peso. How could a rich tourist refuse a poor old Cuban woman, after having just received a free gift from a nice Cuban *señorita*? But I did refuse, and kept on refusing while she kept on insisting. I tried to explain to her in my two-hundred-word Spanish that I don't approve of begging, that I don't believe that beggars are good for Cuba, and that I do give as much as I can afford to, but only to families I know. Not to strangers.

But she wouldn't let me be. She just kept on demanding her peso, and I kept saying *No,* until my friends got tired of this and walked back to the car. When they started opening the doors, I said, *Lo siento* to the woman and left her. Behind my back she unleashed a torrent of angry words.

When I reached the car, I turned around to look at them. From behind the old woman, the young one waved to me.

Previously published in
Haiku Canada Review

Lenin Hospital

My right calf had been sore for more than a week, and yesterday after I had climbed up Cross Hill my leg was swollen from the knee down. I had never had a swollen leg before.

When it remained swollen this morning, in the afternoon, I decided to go to see a doctor after visiting Miriam. She was at the telephone company now, buying herself a cell phone line, after which she would help me to buy Valentine's Day cards. But at 11 o'clock, she phoned that she had been standing in line for an hour and a half, and was already inside the building, but didn't know how long it would be before she'd get out of there, her feet were killing her, and asked me if it would it be all right if she'd help me buy those cards tomorrow morning. Then Carmen showed up, and she and Chiqui and I had lunch. An hour later a tired Miriam walked in.

The three women held a brief conference and decided that Carmen and Miriam would accompany me to the doctor's. According to my Cuban travel health insurance policy, I had to go to a polyclinic on Máximo Gómez Street. Carmen called a friend with a car to drive us there. An attractive young woman doctor saw me almost immediately, looked at my leg, diagnosing it as a, *circulation problem*. She then told us to go to Lenin Hospital for prescriptions.

We caught a horse-driven coach going that way. Thinking of my father who had been a staunch Finnish patriot and anticommunist, I announced that my father would turn over in his grave if he knew that I was going into a Lenin hospital. When the driver and my fellow travelers looked at me with raised eyebrows, I explained that Father had been in the Finnish independence war and that to us Lenin had been the enemy. They all smiled understandingly, and instantly a feeling of friendship was established.

When we reached the hospital, I shook hands with the other passengers and the driver, and Miriam and Carmen grabbed me by the arms and hauled me into the hospital. There, as well as in the polyclinic, the furniture and equipment appeared old-fashioned and timeworn but serviceable, and again I got to see a doctor within a few minutes, and everybody treated me in the most-friendly fashion. The doctor inspected my leg and told us that there was a small blood clot in my vein, and prescribed some cream to put on the leg, and oral medicine. He also wrote instructions on a piece of paper, he gave to Miriam and told me to keep my feet up most of the time and to take it easy until the leg heals.

Then Carmen and Miriam led me to a nearby pharmacy where I bought two small bottles of the medicine to be taken orally, for a total cost of eight pesos. The pharmacy was out of the cream but Carmen promised to find it somewhere else the next day.

Then she walked to wherever she was going next, and Miriam and I caught another horse-driven coach. I descended within two blocks of my house, and Miriam stayed on for the rest of the way to her home.

In the house, Chiqui read the doctor's instructions and gave me my first dose of the oral medicine, and set me on a chair facing another chair with a washbasin of salted water. She lifted my swollen leg on the washbasin, and soaked a towel in the water and placed it on my leg, advising me to sit tight for twenty minutes and keep the towel wet. Then she instructed me to repeat this procedure three times a day, until further notice. And tomorrow morning Carmen would come with the cream and tell me what to do with that.

Previously published in
Haiku Canada Review

About the Author

John Hamley is a retired fisheries scientist and computer salesman who, as Tai puts it, lives nine months of the year like a Cuban in Canada so that in the winter he can live for three months like a Canadian in Cuba. Email:
john.hamley@xplornet.com

Photograph by John Hamley

Photograph by John Hamley

John B. Lee

Encomium

walking the trail
there among bird-foot trefoil
and cow-cress
tall hawkweed and blue chicory
goldenrod spearing out of stone
and the staghorn sumac
its red-velvet seed cone sharp to the sky
with the dying drop-over
of coneflowers
drooping on stems
in the time-bothered pull down
of big-headed summer

what I want of desire
is buzzing weed to weed
with an energetic message of bee's wing
and horsefly hunger
with the active surrender of earth
breaking open
where roots muscle out
at the wind-work
and varmints
dig holes in the dog-nosed scree

and my wife
draws my attention
to the delicate toadflax
through which
I am scuffling
ordinary dancer
on a two-step journey
through blue morning

I am thence in the fold
as a naked companion
of shadow
hiding from God
in this glorious garden
I stand in the flavour of knowledge
with my back to the darkness and my hand to the gate
with its sword

A Bridge for the Horses

my mother lies alone and late
her head sunk in feathers
while clock hands crawl
like locusts in difficult thatches of tall grass
at the coming on of autumn
and she walks the sheets
that wind about her gait like a mourning shroud
with her one hand
tracing the thread count
from within
like a soul with bones

the night that followed
I had a dream
that came to bridge
sunk in a slow river
a bridge set like a puzzle
beneath the flow of clear water
a white bridge that only horses might cross
stepping with care
picking their way
through brilliant spans of man-made stone
an obstacle against interlopers

later we rode through sculptures
which when touched by hooves
rang out with music
melodies composed by angels

and I thought as I woke
of a photograph
of my young mother
when I was the swaddled boy
in her loving arms
and the man who rode with me
gave comfort
in the early hours of the second morning
the blue horizon blooming
in contours of cloud
with the moon on the bay
like the round white forehead of a fading god

A Shorter Row

after her husband passed
the morning glory flourished
in the second summer of sorrow
the blue grief
unfolding the welcome
of time given over
to roses and bone meal
weren't quite so woeful
as emptiness of clothing
and the shaving-brush
morning fragrance in the house

she walked the lawn
in the loud green redolence
of cut clover
and wet gasoline burning
as long as the strength for waking
wasn't too lonesome for rising

attended by daughters
she tended
a shorter row
of green onions and garlic
less parsley
and fewer peas in the colander
unless the grandchildren came
climbing for bings
and the last of the Bartletts
transfigured by sunlight
on the basket by the windowsill

and there she went
as we all do grieving
the winter's ginger-foot sidewalks
and the other long darkness
beginning at four
but the lovely snow solstice comes
dropping cold stars on the tongue

A Sin of Eviction

in the spring
two grackles came and thatched
their nest
upon the upper venting
of a window rattler set high upon our house
and as it is
with the ladder-laziness
of a good man
I gave them squatter's rights
just long enough to warm and
hatch and raise a clutch
of young let fly ... or so I thought
until exigencies
of summer heat required
the cooling of the room
I leaned my will against the wall
and climbed with broom in hand
intent upon eviction
of the dusty mess
that sat like faggots kindled for a fire
I swept the thatching clear
so it flew
and dropped and fell and
wrecked its woody fringes
on the ground
and I, the big wind
of my human will
a god of janitors
or bailiff of the local law
and as I watched
I saw

two fledglings race away
their barely feathered skulls
like balding scholars aging
in a time of war
sad ruin of the animal soul
our stories come to this

go set your sword aside
it's turned to dross and straw.

About the Author

John B. Lee was appointed Poet Laureate of the city of Brantford in perpetuity in 2004 and Poet Laureate of Norfolk County for life in 2015. A member of the Canada Cuba Literary Alliance since its inception, he has visited Cuba on a number of occasions and has written three books of poetry on Cuba, including Sweet Cuba, a book of Cuban poetry translated in collaboration with Manuel Leon and published by Hidden Brook Press in 2010. The four poems are extracts from the book in progress Encomium. Email: johnb.leejbl@gmail.com

Manuel de Jesús Velázquez León

The Silence

In spring, the Silence hid in the basement of the house. It had been concealed for months in between the long weeds that in spring sway slowly with the breeze at the bottom of the lake.

One day, the frosted surface melted. The lake was filled with waves and crashing icebergs. It was then when silence crept up (from) the bushes of the woodland. Between the frozen ground and the snowy roof that piled up over the branches, there was a hidden shadow. There, it found peace for some time.

When the warm rains swept the snow away and the birds filled the woods again with their cacophonic music, silence returned into the basement. Father had left the basement window open to let the fresh March air in, and silence flitted down through the bars, taking shelter in a corner, behind the trunks and the old mattresses. In its hideout, it remained quiet for a long time; there, nothing bothered it.

On Fridays, Milena came to clean. She quickly swept between the rows of bulky boxes and left. Sometimes, Pablo went down into the basement in the morning to explore old stuff in the dusty trunks. He never made a noise, careful not to disturb the silence. Now and then, at dawn, a couple of wary mice and a snake slithered quietly to hide from the world outside.

When the breeze over the woods became warmer and the nights became longer, silence felt that its time had come. It was filled with uneasiness and began to leave its secret hiding place. After supper, when everyone went to bed, it floated up the stairs. Invisible, it slowly engulfed the inner spaces of the house with its soothing calm. It was like the dough for patties that Mother spread with the roller over the marble slab, soft and dry, like the feathers inside a new pillow.

While everyone slept, silence spread and expanded quickly as if lining the walls of the house with feathers. Only time would prevent its growth.

Every hour, the grandfather clock in the hall would burst the silence with its explosive chiming! When the echoes of its chimes faded away, silence reassembled in the air little by little. Every time it recomposed, it had a better defined shape.

In time, silence became more and more daring. It even attempted to escape from the house. One night, it found a crevice in the wall. It reached out with its newly formed legs that quivered with dread as it tried to step into the garden. Despite the cold, there were still crickets hiding within the roots of the sour orange tree. Their chirping cut through its legs and silence had to shrink back into the house.

As twilight came earlier, silence began to leave its shelter before the night began. By then, it had grown long and sluggish wings. It glided slowly, without scattering the dust that covered the furnishings, piled in the basement. In the late afternoon, with an ear against the wall, one could feel the compressed spasms of the air shut in the basement when silence fluttered its wings.

One night, in the small hours, a chill awakened Pablo. Silence was by his side. Crouching besides his bed, it watched the boy with its blind eyes. It enfolded its faded ghostly body with its cottony wings. It held its squalid face within its thin thighs, so lengthy, its knees rose to the ceiling. It wanted to tell him something with its speechless lips, but in the darkness, it was unintelligible. When the boy spoke in his sleep, silence shattered into a cloud of quivering insects that vanished into the dark corners of the room.

Pablo got up and went around the house, opening all the windows for the cold air of the night to seep through. Then, he cuddled within the blankets of his warm bed and slept. He was awakened by a grey calm that came from outside. The birds of dawn were silent. From the window, he saw that, while he slept, silence had covered the meadows and the trees around the house with snow. Pablo looked at the overcast sky; he looked beyond the river. Slowly, the white tide moved away from the house towards the mountainous horizons.

Fishing

Late, every night, mother would wake Pablo and set him to pee on the little red potty so that he learns not to wet the bed anymore. Last night, when Pablo was awakened, he did not complain as usual but hugged and kissed his mother.

Mom, I want to go fishing, Pablo said.

It is night now, baby, she said, *and the fish are sleeping. Tomorrow, I will take you fishing.*

In the morning, mother gave him his bottle as usual, sat him in the high chair and did not say a word about fishing. Pablo began to cry: *You said you would take me fishing!*

Nothing would console or soothe him. Mother was very busy that day. In the backyard, she had all the week's dirty clothes to wash. To keep him happy, she made a fishing rod for Pablo with a bough from the carob tree in the garden, a fragment of sewing yarn and a hooked pin. She put a bucket of water in front of him and submerged one of Milena's old blue shoes inside it. The shoe, with two glass buttons in front and leather ribbons on its sides, closely resembled a fish.

Pablo spent many long hours sitting on his little chair fishing in the bucket. Now and then, he hooked the old blue shoe, *Mom,* he shouted, *I caught it, I caught it!* His mother came, unhooked the prey and returned to her duties in the yard. By mid-morning, as the shoe did not nibble very often, Pablo felt a little sleepy. He held the fishing rod with his left hand and began to suck the two middle fingers of his right hand – the two fingers that he had been sucking since before he was born. He felt his eyes beginning to close. Then, he remembered that he was fishing and was reawakened from his sleep. A little later, he began to suck again – so tasty, those pink little fingers – he struggled to keep his eyes open for a while and finally fell asleep.

Pablo dreamed that it was night and that he was in the woods riding the peacock often depicted in his Dad's stories. The peacock did not jump among the bushes as in the story, but walked slowly and silently because they were fishing. Pablo had a real fishing rod in his hands, a polished fishing rod with the smell of new toy. It had a reel and a crank to rewind the line. Under the trees, coloured fish floated by. Pablo tossed the hook into the shadows.

In the dark corners, big fish opened and closed their gills to the warm air of the night. Eels with shiny scales slowly slid around the tree trunks. Schools of tiny red fish poked about among the leaves, looking for ripe fruit. Long translucent fish swam slowly among the moon rays that filtered through the high branches. While Pablo and his peacock fished, their prey swam close by, looking at them with their crystal eyes, then vanishing into the darkness. Suddenly, something jerked at his line. *Mom, I caught it, I caught it!* In the water of the bucket, hooked to the pin, a blue fish floundered.

Mother has not yet found who the jester was. Meanwhile, in the fish bowl in the living room, an unusual blue fish swims, Milena's old shoe!

If You Make

If you make today a Sunday,
I will tell you of the perfumed shadow
in which that niche of your tenderness left me
where I saw your love bloom in colors
from the humblest things.
If you make gray pink …

We did not know

You did not know your need
nor the extent of your shortage.
The same with me.
I did not know what I craved for,
and I died of hunger,
the hunger I fed on.
Shortage was my affliction.
With you, I can be both man and child.

Not Only

It's not only your beauty,
your greatness;
it is beyond beauty
and the greatness
what you feel for me.

You are Immortal

It is good to discover
time and again
you go beyond your mortal self;
your universe continues
in your imagery,
your smile,
your laugh,
your weeping,
inside my heart,
continues to live on
in my future present.

Invocation

May the gods wish in my woods
you will sleep quietly, fantasy of my dreams;
that your immobile hands may always find me,
for the peace and love I give you,
for the patience to live and then die.
That your flight, nocturnal butterfly,
In my garden continues to perfume the night.

About the Author

Manuel de Jesús Velázquez León is a Professor at the University of Shantou, China. He does research and writes on the English-speaking cultures. For years, Manuel was the Vice-President of the Canada Cuba Literary Alliance and the editor of The Ambassador, the CCLA bilingual magazine. He is also a published poet and writer. Email: manueld@stu.edu.cn

Jennifer Footman

Calling the Kettle Black, Nevada

I amble round Reno bus station
waiting for the bus to the airport.
Cops float, loose hands on holstered guns;
drunks shamble to the edge of the pavement
in a mist of alcohol; a couple of men interrupt a conversation
in Spanish to shout in English that they hate whites, man, they hate whites.
To this pale northerner they look as white as white
as the insipid snow that will be waiting for me
when I return home.

I sit outside on a cool stone wall.
A woman joins me. I guess she too, is Hispanic
because of her black, black hair,
so rich, it could be the glittering body of a raven.
She's about thirty and God, so beautiful
I have to force myself not to stare, not to worship.
She shines, golden-skinned,
ripe as a persimmon about to burst;
her lips bud full, juicy, red without any lipstick;
her eyes glisten a clear, pure, innocent emerald green.
The kind of beauty that is without sex, but is just alive.
A rose in the morning, fresh, mature at the same time.

When she smiles she shows rotten stumps
and three decayed teeth in the upper.
This grey woman, when she smiles, shows perfect white teeth
given to her by luck and the National Health Service.
Though I'm a familiar of the stink of poverty
I enjoy the teeth of the wealthy. The lady in That Play,
she too, knew the acrid fumes as she scrubbed her hands,
scrubbed her hands, scrubbed her hands, trying to erase
the prints of murder. Smile, the world's a happy place.

We chat about buses and her job, her two children
and how buses come, sometimes they don't,
how the evening is the nicest time in Reno.
She says it smells sweet, as honey-like, as golden, as good sex,
the Reno evening. Candied by flowers and night.
The bus arrives in a haze of diesel. We have nothing more to say.
She sits in the front and talks to the driver and I sit in the back.

Previously published: Smoke, UK, 1998
Winner Dorothy Shoemaker Competition, 2013

Akeesha, the One Granddaughter

Through the plastic doors of my shower
I can see your body move.
Your flesh, solid
+one mass under the water,
a waterfall in winter.

The last time I saw you nude
you were six weeks old
and I wondered – this woman of all boys
and many grandsons – at the very positive
female-ness of you. The way
your lips stood proud, red, full.

It seemed to me, that my own boys –
their balls and cock so very prominent –
were men at birth. That *thing* hard,
sticking out, the balls turgid
ready, as if waiting to be emptied.

Your six-year-old body is not quite
tall enough to reach the control
and I have to adjust it and wait for you
to finish. You wash your hair,
rub the shampoo into it.
You soap your body, slightly opening your legs
rubbing and rinsing, letting the water flow
where it will.

This pink shadow
moves with a grace,
a rhythm
hard to soft
quick to slow, in its languid heaviness.
I would love to live long enough
to see you pregnant
heavy, full, that fine body a receptacle for love.

Previously published: ones Avenue, Canada, 2001

Local Interest Brampton: Holy Man

A sadhu picks as his perch, a quiet spot
in the small park near my house.
He stands just out of the shade of a maple
as if he craves the sun on his skin,
its rays an extra stave for beating his flesh.

Veiled in dust from head to toe,
postured on one leg,
he turns into a powder statue.

He stares ahead, dazed,
there and not there, his glazed, blank eyes
dead fish flat.
Flies cover his lips;
ants climb his leg and he never moves.

Every now and then, a dog will stop,
sniff, move on as if searching for something
that is vital, alive. This man has no stink
of human or dog, but has mastered a thing
created from atoms of carbon
lined up in random fashion without core or centre.

His torn clothes flap against him,
even on the stillest days.
White ribs shine through mahogany skin
while pelvic bones push through his body.
His long matted, red-mudded hair hangs to his waist.
Black holy beads and ropes
circle his neck and wrists.

A passing man flicks flies
from the sadhu's face, strokes ants
off his leg. The sadhu gives no sign
of pleasure or gratitude.

In winter too, he stands beside the maple,
covered from neck to toe in down,
shoeless, his hands blue, his head shining
he continues his meditation
as if the world is dead
and he nothing but a ghost.

Grand-daughter

If you were mine, I'd pray
for your face to be plain
as rock. Let no beauty taint

you, nor curse you with leaden
eyes or airy skin; be furnished with bare
essentials to snail along a candid path.

If you would listen to me
I'd cover you in sack-cloth and ashes,
bid you be invisible as new-cleaned glass.

If I had you, I'd banish make-up, you would pipe
no surface icing onto your skin,
nor starve yourself thin

as a tall column of iced water
for a man to spill and waste,
with his exacting breath.

Puritan, I'd expel Cavaliers.
For thee, plain grey to blanket curves;
white, to dull the colour in your cheeks.

Let a man love you, adore you, crave
you, regard you, relish you, burn
for you just for your manifest naked grace.

Previously published: Gathering Fuel

Beavering about in an Ontario Fall

Tripping along a wooded path,
townee ignorant, thick as a turtle's
shell, I admire trees and birds,
trilliums and chipmunks, while I'm eaten alive
in spite of Deep Woods Off.

At a beaver dam, in mid-swat, I stop.
Rods, twigs and logs regiment
to create a wall high above the road
while on the still water a loon bleats.

Sticks and stones can break no bones
in this cottony shade where pines gather hair
and blood fills bodies of fat blackflies.

I lean on a rock, a bit concerned in case
I disturb some private beaver ritual.

The smell of clay and moss weighs
like lead in my head and in my arid mouth
the guilty sting of wine from lunch.

Tons of water held by this dam
made of wood and mountains of mud
change me into an ant, a fly, or a gnat
in front of this monument to work, work, work.

March, you foolish beavers, march,
break out of dams, flood roads;
tramp to win my soft world,
surround me with moons and rampant loons.
Pretty please, damn me close to you.

I will slip into your skins, your tight, dense
pelts as easily as a bored hunter
skins a pair of dead beaver.

Leave your grave water, follow
the snakes into hollow
gaps in rock. Beavers, whisper,
so only I hear your song
in the black core of the lake

About the Author

Originally from India, Jennifer Footman spent most of my life in Edinburgh and am a graduate of that university, coming to Canada in 79. My poetry and fiction have been in most Canadian literary magazines and many US and UK ones. I have three collections of poetry. Email: Jbfootman@yahoo.ca

Colin Morton

Five to Midnight

At last the storm is passing, or pausing
to restore itself over the gulf, clouds heave
a redolent breath on the rooftops
and behind the closed door, your howls
have ended,
       sleep
washes anger and fear from your face.

I stand over your bed, twenty years
from an understanding with you,
knowing we may not have those years
or if we do, today
will be dream time then to both of us,
become other people, translated
into foreign lives

You won't remember this day and I
might say nothing happened.
We made it through the hours at home
on the bus and on
the hate/love rollercoaster ride of being five.
I listened to the news at lunch, dreading
to be out of touch another hour.
We put together your jigsaw puzzles
to show you had all the pieces;
you did a lot for yourself, even without
me in the end,
       as you will have to
some day we can't yet imagine.

The sky is impatient, tugged and tossed
in a mist of last roses
        and above the rain,
satellites plough silent cameras through
what is left of the twentieth century

almost everywhere on earth is tomorrow.

Previously published:
Coastlines of the Archipelago,
Buschek Books, Canada

For Now

They walk in and out of your life till
without noticing you begin to rely
on them, going in and out. You notice
when you realize some have gone
out of your life one last time and you
won't see them again, or if you do,
it is lifetimes later on a busy corner
and neither can find a thing
to say more than anything else right now
and so they say goodbye.
         You are not
inconsolable. You know how it feels
to go out of people's lives and
not come back. Sometimes, it is
deliberate. Usually though
it is this same daily passing of things
(our minds are always on about what we
are about to receive). And there are
always others, walking in and
out of your life, but now you
notice it a little more, you begin
shaking hands, even with friends,
hugging, touching, lingering in doorways
talking about nothing much, anything,
not wanting to say goodbye just yet.

Previously published:
How to Be Born Again,
Quarry Press, Canada

Night-walking Between Centuries

Somewhere between ends and beginnings
alert to the scuff of a shoe in the shadows
a block away, I walk the night streets
of this city midway through self-demolition
half-metamorphosed half-decayed –
passing shadows of my former self
on streets where storefronts have shifted,
signs altered, brick facades from another century
caught in a bank tower's funhouse mirrors.

And turning a corner I sometimes glimpse
the virtual, the becoming city
as near in time as this red brick,
though barely imagined here at street level,
where for years I've crossed against the light
and soon the first trans-humans will cross,
become one with their appliances.

At the edges of vision, they pass like shadows
eyes never meeting, as if they don't see me
or if they do, do not see me as forebear
flat-footed, astigmatic, fatally flawed –
an X of flesh in a world of unknowns,
caught in reflection between walls of glass.

Previously published:
The Local Cluster,
Pecan Grove Press, Canada

Black Ice

You didn't see this coming but
there's no way to back out now

Steer into the skid
look for traction on snow

Don't lock the brakes or it's all
gone to smash

Have matches, candles, blankets with you
if you're stuck in a snow bank

That blocks the exhaust
don't run the motor for heat

Open the door if you can
breathe fresh cold air

Look up and be glad
you can see the stars

Previously published:
Winds and Strings,
BuschekBooks, Canada

About the Author

Colin Morton is a Canadian poet living in Ottawa. He has been a publisher and editor (Ouroboros), a spoken-word performer (First Draft), a film producer (Primiti Too Taa), a novelist (Oceans Apart), a reading series director (Tree), vice-president of the League of Canadian Poets, and author of ten books of poetry. Many of his poems have been translated into Spanish by Manuel de Jesus Leon. Email: colinmorton@sympatico.ca

Photograph by John Hamley

Photograph by Richard M. Grove

Photograph by Wency – Wenceslao Alexander Rosales

Photograph by Wency – Wenceslao Alexander Rosales

Photograph by John Hamley

Photograph by John Hamley

Chris Faiers

Five Minutes Ago they dropped the Bomb – 1984

After the bomb dropped
the homophobic cop
and the steam-bath patron he was handcuffing
melted into each other's arms
into infinity

After the bomb fell
concrete angels in all the graveyards
took wing
Every bell in the world
gave one last high-pitched ring into oblivion

Five minutes ago
a tear or two slipped in the halls of karma
at the insignificant passing of
3rd. dimensional existence –
3rd. stone from the sun – reality factor
time factor irrelevant –
total dissolution of creatures
   IQ 100   EQ 35
evolutionary phase median ape to bodhisattva

The bodhisattvas wept
Buddha watched mountains raise their final crest –
burst into pulverized space/time

Basho's spirit watched every moment in nature
cruelly bloom into the final haiku moment of infinity

Five minutes ago
the Marxists got their final synthesis
the Neo-Nazis their final solution
the capitalists their last boom from the economy

Five minutes ago we kissed
said "Shit! They've done it ..."
Armageddon – Apocalypse

Five minutes ago Time Must Have a Stop
five minutes ago we passed into borrowed time
five minutes multiplied 12 times by the hour
24 times by the day
365 times by the year
and 38 times since Hiroshima shimmered into oblivion

Five minutes ago we passed into borrowed time again
reality factor minus:
3 million
994 thousand
and sixty

five minutes ago

Author's note

> *This poem was multi-published in 1984 – in the following:*
> *Five Minutes Ago they dropped the Bomb Chapbook*
> *The Unfinished Anthology (Unfinished Monument Press),*
> *Anti-War Poems: an anthology edited by Stehen Gill (Vesta Publications)*
> *The Americas Review Magazine*
> *Republished in Crossing Lines: Poets Who Came to Canada in the Vietnam War Era, Allan Briesmaster and Steven Michael Berensky, (Seraphim Editions, 2008).*
> *War-era poets share experiences, Toronto Star review of Crossing Lines by Joe Fiorito*
> *Flipping thru anthologies and books which have included my poems, today I discovered several more credits for this poem*
> *Foot Through the Ceiling, 1986, Aya Press (now Mercury Press) collection for which I received the inaugural Milton Acorn People's Poetry Medal in 1987*
> *The Last blewointment Anthology, edited by bill bissett, 1985, Nightwood Editions*
> *Keeper of the Conscience (anthology), edited by Ronald Kurt and Mark McCawley, 1990, Greensleeve Publishing*
> *Other Channels (anthology), edited by Shaunt Basmajian and jones, 1984*
> *Waves (magazine), Vol. 13, No. 1, Fall 1984, pages 76 – 77*
> *Piping at the End of Days: A book of Overcoming (anthology), edited by Katherine L. Gordon, 2017 Valley Press, Rockwood, Ontario.*

Solstice morning:
smudge smoke in my hair
hoarfrost on every tree

Winter Solstice Smudging 2005

Had a great smudging ceremony last night, although it's obviously more fun when Morley joins me. Stated the fire around 11 pm, & had to break a trail to the chiminea thru a foot of snow. I've gotten so good at starting winter fires, even when my wood is covered in snow, that I had the chiminea roaring in 10 minutes. Had a large, almost empty bottle of Pelee Island chiraz, & made several (many?) trips back inside to take a sip & get warm while I waited for midnight. It was by far the coldest of the 3 Solstice ceremonies so far.

At midnight, I did my usual ritual ringing in the 4 points of the compass, & got to use my spiffy new Tibetan bell – great strong sound! Then smudged in incense & rich smoke from the white pine boughs I collected on Monday's hike. When I awoke this morning it took a second or 2 to realize the great smoky aroma was in my hair :) Always feel refreshed & purified after the Solstice ceremony. When I looked out the window at noon all the trees were covered in white hoarfrost!

Note by the author:
Sorrow Falls – just off the Trans-Canada Trail near Marmora, Ontario (pix yesterday) by Dr. John, who named the smaller set of icicles, "The Shaman's Whiskers"

About the Author

Chris Faiers is a Canadian poet who has been at the forefront in the development of English language, haiku and haibun since 1967. He has been internationally published in dozens of publications, Unfinished Monument Press, Main Street Library Poetry, ZenRiver Gardens and PurdyFests. He has created the concept of, emotional intelligence in this 1984 poem/movie script being developed, Eel Pie Island Dharma by Hidden Brook Press, Canada.Email: zenriver@sympatico.ca

Miriam Estrella Vera Delgado

Bird of Love

A Bird of Love came
Flying
And perched on a birch
Tree;
I thought Love had
Arrived,
It had remembered me.
But Love was only
Resting,
Didn't even look at me;
Love opened its wide
Wings
And flew over the Sea;
It fled over the Ocean ...
Love didn't remember
Me.

Life

Life is to us a Mystery
Like a magician's hat,
One minute can mean happiness
The next, your worlds collapse.
When it comes to fortune
It takes you up and down,
One day you are a peasant
Next day you wear a crown.
Like a roller coaster
Your happiness soars high,
Then it just plummets down
Because you lived a lie.
Other times you're full of joy
You laugh aloud you dance,
You feel just like a child
On a Merry-go-Round.
But do not be deceived
You never know what lies in wait,
One minute you are flying:
The next you are grief-stricken,
You are crying.

Destiny is a Train

Our life is like a journey
We start on when born,
We go to towns and cities
And want to travel more.
We're riding on a train,
A train that always stops;
We choose our destination
And this determines our fate.

But if we can choose what's right
Life will be filled with joy,
And our future will be bright.
But if our choice is wrong
We will suffer and regret.
I myself have long endured
The hardships of my errors
So when the next stop is in sight
I'll be hoping to choose right
And that this time round,
My happiness will be found.

A Bird at my Window

A bird at my window,
Flutters its wings;
The pretty bird at my window,
It chirps and sings.
Do you bring a message,
My joyful, little friend?
Did you get your tune
From someone else,
Or is it an angel's message?
Still I cannot comprehend
What you are saying:
Do you live nearby,
Or far away in heaven?
Oh pretty bird, my little friend
Are you the hope I need?
Maybe you bring a message
Perhaps love's sweet essence?

Loneliness

I drink from it every night:
This loneliness is like vinegar,
Its sharp sour taste
Lingered in my mouth
For the past decade.
Sometimes it feels sweetly acidic
Then it turns pungently bitter;
From this, my solitude is triggered!

About the Author

Recipient of various literary awards, Miriam Estrella Vera Delgado is from Holguin. She writes poetry in Spanish and in English. Her poetry was featured in, Stellar Showcase Journal (2009). Her book, From the Heart published by Graham Publishing, Canada, 2010. Her work was published in Canada Cuba Literary Alliance publications: The Ambassador, Envoy and anthologies and in Spain.

George Elliott Clarke

On the Martyrdom of Malcolm X
(pace Bobby Burns)

Stagnant now's the blood whence it stood and stained;
Fled his killers whence his mourners remained,
Careless before his carefree cadaver.
Malcolm X has now entered *Forever*.

Beautifully ugly fell *Catastrophe*;
Zeroed in bullets so the hero'd see.
Charismatic even as he collapsed,
Malcolm X thrived as mortal Malcolm lapsed.

Bright flared gunfire; earthy pounded the blasts.
The *Death*-sentenced saint fell back a carcass.
Zesty, his eyeglasses sparked and splintered.
Now a ghost, Malcolm X won't be interred.

Assassins squeezed out doors and squeezed through screams.
Cancers blighted *Love*; nightmares blacked-out dreams.
Mourners blamed C.I.A., and cried out, "Why?!!"
Malcolm X crisscrossed spot-lit sky.

All that Sunday morn, there'd been plenty hint
The orator'd die. One moment vibrant,
The next disappeared, unable to live,
Malcolm X knew *Death* as preservative.

Nobodies shot him down; their graves are mud.
Flowerless endlessly, their corpses leak crud.
Eminently beloved, Malcolm X lives –
Wherever *Liberty* forever thrives.

Judas 1-10

A mackerel stench soaked our house.
Christ! My people were gutter trash.

A filthy, yellow-eyed bitch,
mama accomplished *Virginity* –
just turned up her sore, dripping asshole.

That unsmiling whore wed a man
almost too scabrous to jack off,
but everybody licks cunt.
Yep, everybody.

I grew up – mongrel mid monsters.
Pops – a career drunk; Ma – a 24/7 slut.
At cocksucking,
each did a bang-up job.

Nightly, I watched Mr. kneel
at mistress's gash
as much as she liked,
and use her again and again.

They gratified each other crisply,
and customers too.
Our kitchen come a sperm factory.

One gent exited mom,
and, laughing, spunked on my forehead.

Glad I was when my folks conked out,
jointly stabbed,
their last, foul breaths heating each other's asses.

Tis a good thing that The Creator
is awful skilled at killing.

He's a necessary *Terror* –
Ally – for spawn like me.

[Udine (Italy) 28 avril/Nisan mmxi]

The Book of Samson
(Repressed Excerpt from Judges)
IV.

Screed 2

Adultery is a savage institution —
Marriage gone gamey —

so that ladies of frank hindquarters —
in ravishing draperies —

a belligerent harem —
convert husbands to monkeys,

a mirage regime,
wherein philosophers talk shit and eat it too.

[Frankfurt (Germany) 22 décembre mmx]

Screed 3

Regular servings
of liquor and *queynte* —

us stiffen —
as if in a coffin.

Don't let go of wine!
To be an ascetic is to suffer an undeveloped character.

*[Frankfurt (Germany) 22 décembre mmx
& New York (New York) 20 janvier mmxi]*

About the Author

The 4th Poet Laureate of Toronto, (2012-15) and the 7th Poet Laureate of Canada (2016-17), George Elliott Clarke Is revered for his unusual conjunctions of Black English and Queen's English. A Nova Scotian, Clarke teaches African-Canadian Literature at the University of Toronto. His books appear in Chinese, Italian, and Romanian. Email: torontopoetlaureate@gmail.com

K.V. Skene

Accidental Purpose

I take long walks,
listen to ghosts – how little they say,

how soon I forget, will be forgotten,
buried beneath October leaf-litter

as lovers huddle on park benches, plot-
tomorrows and more tomorrows ...

A hunter's moon bleeds through thin branches,
night shadows shiver

around corners, leap trash bins, dodge lampposts
and glacier-blue memories solidify,

into assertive adolescences – blasphemous
in their callowness, their credulity, their overt

curiosity and I lose myself. Not quite
deliberately. Not quite willfully.

More like a mistake I've been wanting
to make.

Previously published – Acumen 84, January 2016 (UK)

Cold Comfort

the first winter starts with our shoes
as mornings slow-shift

focus on toes and fingertips
bite down

if we look too long
the day will fool us and snow

will fall and paper leaves and pine needles
rise over whitened rooftops

frost-rimed foxes scavenge
in bins and tender wrens hungrily

berrying the bitter holly
take what is theirs

of course the weather worsens
we have known children

not unlike ourselves
who fail to follow their footprints

all the way back home
but we are quietly confident

a sensible sliver of January sun
pins everything in place

a kiss
trapped between two mouths

can ripen
in fresh fallen snow

and one of us falls backwards
grows the wings of an angel

one of us
has never been this way before or since

Previously published – Weyfarers, No. 105, January 2009 (UK)

Climate Change

a rising wind
cuts over
the breakwater
quick-frozen
our first storm
this winter
bent on becoming
worse

solid
pack ice
up ahead
unseasonable
damages
split a community
first to endure bad
things

as a steel blade
shatters
the future is
cold
disproportionally
and every heart
breaks
could happen

*Previously published – NÔD,
Issue No. 9, January 2009 (Canada)*

All the walls close in and the day …

folds into its envelope – thin, tarnished,
more tenuous than ever before. The glass is empty,
the book marked, the fire banked
as the house settles into its plot. Now face
the icy hardwood floor, slippery stairs
as hallway, landing, bathroom, bedroom
furnish their own weather and those memories
that drift underneath the duvet
as you struggle to sleep …
                     In the morning
the walls will expand with each breath,
spill into the hall
before you. The suitcases,
ready and waiting, will commence the countdown
and the taxi will come.

Previously published – Reach Poetry,
165, June 2012 (UK)

About the Author

K.V. Skene's poetry has been published in Canada, the U.K., U.S.A, Ireland, India, Australia and Austria magazines Her publications include Love in the (Irrational) Imperfect, Hidden Brook Press, 2006 (Canada) You Can Almost Hear Their Voices, Indigo Dreams Publishing (UK) and Under Aristotle Bridge, 2015, Finishing Line Press (USA). Email: kv.skene@bell.net

Connie Kinnell McKinney

The Hawk Tree

As soon as we knew the danger had passed, my family and I emerged from the safety of our basement and looked outside to survey the damage. There was still a light rain falling, and, like the droplets of rain coursing down our windows, there was suddenly something inside me that wanted to cry. It was instantly apparent that our back yard would never look the same again. A spring tornado had just passed south of us, but the outer bands had been strong enough to whip our trees around with little mercy. One large tree had fallen and numerous other limbs and leaves were scattered everywhere.

My family and I had moved to Carthage, Missouri just two years earlier. We loved the home we found nestled in a wooded acreage along Center Creek. I have always loved the woodlands and the beautiful side of nature. It is God's cathedral to me and, to my way of thinking, it is the best place to be whenever possible. However, this day seemed to show only the harsh and brutal side of the outdoors I loved. A part of me broke with the broken-down tree. The next day, my husband, David, cleared away as much debris as possible, trimmed off the branches from the fallen tree and left only its main trunk to be sawed into firewood later. It was then that my heart broke even more. Only after the debris was gone did I see it …

Normally, our neighborhood is gloriously beautiful in the spring with an abundance of Dogwood trees in bloom. It looks like a picture out of fantasyland for the few weeks they are blooming. Now, however, it was clear that one of my favorite Dogwood trees had been nearly destroyed by the fallen tree. This beautiful, fragile tree had grown with two main trunks spreading into a "V" shape. Every year I had looked forward to watching this particular tree unfold its blossoms upon its slender branches – glorious, delicate spots of color, as if suspended in air in a crowning glory. Now, I could see that the trunk leaning to the left looked unscathed, while the trunk to the right had been broken off where the branches with it blossoms had been; leaving what looked to me like an ugly stick, with just a little jutting, broken piece of a branch left.

Broken ... ugly ... useless ... never as good as before ... were just some of the phrases that wove through the emotions of my disappointment. Why did it have to happen to *that* tree? Why did the storm have to hurt, break and ruin the beauty of *that* tree? I wanted to go out and saw down that now ugly reminder of something beautiful that was taken from me. The sight of it hurt me and I wanted to remove it, yet, at the same time, I knew that the feelings in my heart, or this little tree would ever, or could ever be the same again. Both of us were changed forever. "Life" happened. It wasn't the little tree's fault. It wasn't the fallen tree's fault. It wasn't even the storm's fault, but I could find no consolation in the wake of its aftermath.

Frankly, I just didn't want to think about it. My "normal self" had been disrupted and I was angry. My inner child was having a huge self-pity party. I had suffered loss but could take no vengeance. Was I being unreasonable? Yes, no doubt. After all, my family was safe and our home untouched. I had much to be thankful for. Life moved on.

For one reason or another, I never did get around to sawing down the broken trunk of my Dogwood tree. Perhaps, I knew that my pain and disappointment would still be there. The feeling of loss would still be there. The beauty that I once enjoyed would never return. Yes, it was depressing to look at my "ugly stick", day after day. Still, I left it alone. Something, or rather I, now know, someone, held me back from trying to change the unchangeable. I just did not yet have the eyes to see what He saw.

Epilogue

It is my habit to take my coffee and my Bible and spend some quiet time with my Lord in the morning, out in our sunroom, on the back of our home. It is my special place. It is there that I watch the world wake up, where the birds come to feed, the river flows gently by and the flowers bloom. And I pray.

Since the storm, my routine continued with one exception. Yes, I would pray, but then I would look up and see my *ugly stick*. There was no escaping the truth of it. It was as stuck as I was in our shared brokenness.

One day, as I was praying, I asked God to explain me why my little tree had been destroyed? Why it had been disfigured into an *ugly stick*? How could I ever get over the feeling of loss and disappointment that had unsettled my world? At that very moment, in the middle of my prayer, the *broken* turned into *beautiful* as a magnificent, majestic hawk flew down and used the little jutting part of my "ugly stick" as a perch. In an instant, my little tree took on a new look and a different purpose – one that I could have never imagined.

I was in awe as I studied that beautiful creature. For a few moments, he just sat there – at full attention, vigilant and proud – like a king watching over his kingdom. It was almost as if he had come just for me, to give me hope and a new perspective through his eyes; his beautiful, sharp and true hawk eyes. In that moment, my little tree found new meaning and purpose. A warm, breathing, feathered creature now crowned the broken tree where blossoms would never grow again. Somehow, the beauty of the present replaced the destruction of the past. Somehow, in that moment, the sadness in my heart went away and was replaced with new hope and anticipation that the bird, and others like him, would return to be admired again and again. Somehow, in that instant, I began to see through different eyes, His eyes – the eyes of our Redeemer, who can make *all things new*.

Sooner or later, each and every one of us is subjected to *life's cruelty* happening to us. Our lives are turned upside down by a loss of some kind. We lose a job, or a loved one. We make a wrong choice and reap the consequences. We hurt someone, or someone hurts us. We become broken ... never to be the same again. Like the broken branch of the Dogwood, ripped from its original form, we are changed and mourn the loss. We wonder, then question: *How could any good ever come from this?*

Time is a gift and it brings a lot of healing beyond the grieving. It is good, but it cannot redeem nor restore a loss. That is all right. We take each gift for what it is. But sometimes, we need more. We need hope, enough hope to let go what can never be the same again. A hope that releases enough faith to ask God to open our eyes to see as He sees things. Yes, eyes that can see how the future can be.

What has been cannot be changed, but the future can bring unimagined beauty and purpose. Honestly, in a million years, I would have never thought about parting the Red Sea, or walking on water. Would you? My mind is too small to wrap around such wonders. Moreover, my mind is too small to know how to fix anything beyond changing a light bulb, let alone a broken heart. The only thing any of us can do at such times, is to pray and ask our Redeemer, our Savior, to come and do what only He can do – perform *a miracle just made just for us.* He who created the tree and the hawk has the power and imagination to do just that. Moreover, He wants to.

My little Dogwood tree will remain as it is, as long as we live here. The hawk still stops by to survey his kingdom from time to time, and I can only smile. Joy has replaced my sadness. I have my miracle. He will do no less for you ...

Like my heart, the little tree has found a new beginning. No longer is it simply my favorite Dogwood tree. It is my Hawk Tree.

Birdie Weaver

Have you ever been tempted to question the wisdom of God? To be honest, I have. To be very honest, I have questioned His judgement several times in my walk with Him. And yet, almost as often, in His infinite patience with me, He has surprised me and sent answers my way, explaining *the why* of some things to me. One such time was when I met Birdie Weaver.

Several years ago, my husband and I thought it would be a kindness to go and walk the halls of a local nursing home, just to take away some of the lonely time that so many endure there. Even well – meaning friends and family could not fill in all the hours of their day to day existence. Sadly, a few had no friends, or family to come see them. We hoped we could fill in the gap a little, as we went from one room to another, just to sit and chat for a few moments with some of the residents. It was in one of these rooms that I found Birdie.

Faint sunlight filtered through the window by her bed, resting softly on her tiny form curled in a fetal position. When she saw me enter the room, she turned her head upward toward me happily, but at the same time, a bit cautiously. I think she was surprised to have a visit from a stranger and was probably trying to size up this person that had walked into her small world. Tiny and frail, I was trying to size her up as well. To my shame, I hastily decided, I probably wouldn't take away much from our visit. In one grand, self-righteous moment, I looked at the "cover" of this book and decided it probably wasn't worth reading for very long. Still, she invited me to sit down, which I did, and we began to talk. The book of her life was opened…and God smiled. I didn't know it then, but I was going to be blessed, despite my hasty assessment of this tiny senior citizen.

It has been said that, "dynamite comes in small packages". Little did I know that I was about to be "blown away" by what I would discover in Birdie. No, she was not the feisty kind of personality, but rather, the deep and profound kind – deeper and sweeter, than I ever could have imagined.

As I talked with Birdie, I expected a frail mind to match her frail body. I was pleasantly surprised to find the opposite. She was intelligent and articulate and a joy to talk to. In the course of our conversation, she pointed to a notebook on a table by her bed and offered to let me read some of the entries. She was a poetess and the notebook, which looked as worn and unassuming as its owner, contained some of her poems. I had also written some poems and was somewhat curious to discover what lay within the pages of her book. Yet, again, in my small-mindedness, I wasn't expecting much; hoping at best for a "Jack and Jill" type of writing. I was immediately humbled and very pleasantly surprised as I began to read her verses.

Her words were rich and deep, well written and eloquent, simple and profound, mature and yes, even inspiring. I was in the presence of greatness and I almost passed her by. The "cover" of her life in no way drew attention to the richness of her content. I was so glad I took the time to get a glimpse into part of her life.

Prior to meeting Birdie, I had one question that had always haunted me. From time to time, I would wonder why God would keep some people here longer than (it seemed to me) they should be? When years were well spent, when one's body was worn and weary, when one felt their life no longer had meaning or purpose, I would ask, "Wouldn't it make more sense to take this one home a little sooner, Lord?"

I don't think the Lord minds when we ask such questions. This is how we learn. This is how we grow. I believe the Lord delights in helping us do both.

As I rose to leave, I knew I would never be the same person as before. I came to be a blessing to Birdie, but in turn, walked away blessed. From that moment on, I would try my best to never make too quick of an assessment of what was inside a person, nor of their value, however long their journey on this earth was. It was not for me to make such a call.

I have learned, as long as we draw breath, we have purpose. I have learned that no matter what our circumstances might appear to be, we can be useful and plant seeds of goodness and kindness in others; seeds of a good and wise Creator to grow in the hearts we touch. As it was with Birdie and me, she would never know her life would change mine forever.

Not long after our visit, I learned that Birdie had passed away. I will never forget her. My eyes and my heart were opened a little wider through the life of that frail, tiny lady in a passing moment in my life. I learned my lesson well and, even now, I try daily to look beyond the surface of a person to see what is really in their heart ... all because of what little Birdie once taught me those many years ago.

About the Author

Connie Kinnell McKinney grew up in NY and MA before attending Cottey College in Nevada, MO. Connie has written inspirational articles for two newspapers and several poems. She currently resides in Springfield, MO with her husband, David. She enjoys spending time with their four children and their families.
Email: c.mckinney57@yahoo.com

Eugenio Ernesto González Aguilera

To Gibara

You still dream of the waves lapping
against the hill that looms over your shores;
they contemplate your feeble structures
intent on outliving the surrounding auras.
They say you lie still in your oblivion
and no offspring shall come from your entrails,
they say that your fertile bright soul
today no longer shines.
White Villa, fishermen´s passion;
your roofs, your waves, your greenness
are signatures of your unique sweetness.
Call out your name to those who forgot you,
come back to life, like the Phoenix,
you, the eternal deity of sea and adventure.

To the Bellomar Hotel
(Home of the Quintana family)

Standing before a blurred vision
        no sea no skies –
in pulsating sleeplessness
the soul of the house sighs;
no miracle befalls it
no promise of fortune;
the desolate house revisits
its past in its present derelict state,
same as the town that doesn't remember
in its oblivious and demented ruin.

To the Gibara Saddle

The sky surrounds you
above the briny tang of the sea;
you stand before shore and wind
your silhouette survives.
A Gibara of ocean blue
on the Bay´s backgrounds,
the mysterious Saddle
baptized by the Admiral
like a luminescent jewel
amidst the heart of the Villa.

About the Author

Eugenio Ernesto González Aguilera is a poet from Gibara and has a Bachelor´s Degree in Sociocultural Studies. Member of the Iberianamerican Group of the Cucalambé Décima and the Artistic and Literary Group of Gibara, He received several literary awards. His work has been published locally and in several Canada Cuba Literary Alliance publications.

Debbie Carpenter

My Small Hand in Hers

When I was young Mom took my hand,
For glad adventures she had planned.
Off to the park to play in the sand,
How joyous those times were.
Then to the library we would go,
Where all the books stood in a row.
We'd read them with our eyes aglow,
My small hand in hers.

At Christmastime we'd go downtown
We'd hear the bells, oh what a sound,
With merry shoppers all around,
And decorated firs.
We'd eat in a café, what great fun!
Times like these were next to none.
We'd head for home when day was done
My small hand in hers.

Seasons come seasons go,
And all too quickly I did grow.
How time flew I'll never know,
It all seems like a vision blurred.
Often I spent time with my friends,
Yet on Mom's love I could depend,
Still time together we would spend,
My hand now next to hers.

A good man came into my life,
Asking me shyly to be his wife.
But that did not cause Mom much strife,
Instead her heart with love was stirred.
Children were born and she'd ask me,
And all my family to come for tea.
A family we would always be
Now, their small hands in hers.
 Then came the day by Mother's bed,
I heard the words the doctor said:
When my heart was filled with dread,
We didn't have much time.
I thought about the days gone by,
And as the tears filled my eyes,
She crossed the path to heaven's skies.
Her cold hand in mine.

Previously published: Hidden Brook Press,
Grandmother, Mother, and Me.

Since Skippy came to Stay

Our little home was quiet,
And we would always stop,
To look at other people's dogs,
 When we went for a walk.
We felt something was missing,
What was it – we could not say:
But everything has changed
Since Skippy came to stay.

Skippy is part terrier,
And part schnauzer too.
His feet are like a Dachshund,
He's a darling through and through.
He's certainly an active pup,
Loves to run and play.
Our home is not so quiet
Now that Skippy's came to stay.

Skippy likes to teeth on things,
So he had to be taught.
To munch on little chewy toys,
Not new furniture we bought.
His toys are strewn all through the house,
He leaves them just that way,
We do a lot of picking up,
Since Skippy came to stay.

We find him outside eating bugs,
Or biting our fingers;
The vet costs us a fortune,
But still we love his vigor.
He's really rather fond of us,
Tries his hardest to obey.
Cuddles up in the evening,
Now that he's come to stay.

He can be good, or very naughty,
This I know for fact.
But then I think he's special makes him,
Fill the day with happiness to the brim.
And when I wake up in the morning,
To start my chores every new day,
I'm ever so very grateful
Little Skippy's come to stay.

Skippy posing for a photo in the garden

About the Author

Debbie Carpenter enjoys writing and watching University of Arizona basketball games with her husband. She is a devoted mother of two daughters, son in-laws, and five grandchildren and member of the Canada, Cuba Literary Alliance. She lives in Tucson, USA. Email: Newvistas3@cox.net

Dorothy Cox Rothwell

The Woods on a Winter Night

Motionless i stand at the edge of the woods:
    alone i enter deep into you
unafraid, plunging into your whiteness,
    your tranquility
broken only by the snapping of a branch
or my footsteps breaking the crust of snow.
The winter moon lays solemn
    in the frost-black winter sky
pearl-white, luminous;
silvery moonbeams filtering
    over the winter scene
making it unreal, mystical haunting,
casting long dark shadows of trees
    Suddenly i am a child again:
light headed with joy and wonder
at the beauty of a sparkling enchanting moment;
the woods on a moonlit winter night
    unforgettable.

The World is Square/Round
the world man makes is square;
we live in square houses
that look like salt boxes
with square windows to look out on the world,
square rooms with square tiles
on the floor,
square tables to eat on
rectangular beds and cribs
for our babies;
and even the caskets we're buried in
lowered into rectangular holes
have square markers to tell we were here.
But God has made the natural things round

the sun and moon,
the earth itself
round heads, breasts, mouths,
holes in the earth
and things that grow upon it,
tree trunks, oranges, apples
eggs with yellow rounds yolks,
life itself springs from an egg
and grows into a human being:
to experience all this
hard edged, square linear
world created by man.

Inscape 111

I travel without a map
making my way
across the inscape.

There are no pictures
nothing to look at
only records
there, I have it
centuries and people
are watching my inner journey
searching for the path.

Here and now
I love,
suffer, sigh, weep
am happy in grief,
nothing matters
but the poem,
my life
a record of searching,
struggle, pain,
sometimes joyful moments
and that is my existence
now.

Fire
I want to be fire
that burns old wood
and leaves giving off
the smell of wood smoke,
dancing tantalizing
consuming flames, flickering
dying, smouldering
to become grey ashes
warm cool.

Letting go

My memories
are like torn sheets
threadbare, ragged
beyond repair
discoloured by time
greyed and yellowed
fading
soon to be discarded.

About the Author

Dorothy Cox Rothwell is a Spiritualist Minister, Writer, Poet and works in healing arts. Her work has appeared in Portraits, by Peterborough Area Women Past and Present, the Otonabee Tapestry, Poetry Box, Parachute, Sacred Encounters with Mary, Grandfather, Father and Me and The Link Magazine. She is member of the Writer Group, 7ish.
Email: dotcox@cogeco.ca

Hugh Hazelton

Amigo
for Walter Amaral

the news
came yesterday
pulmonary embolism
he died almost immediately
in his apartment
before he could even get
to the phone

your forthright eyes
sense of humour
firm handshake when I'd arrive
and your *Bem-vindo, amigo! Como vai?*
the stories of your travels
your years as a Jesuit brother
bringing liberation
to the burnt villages of the Northeast
and classrooms of São Paulo
years studying architecture in Poland
crazy times as a tourist guide in the Yucatán
and arrival in Montreal
to spread the word
of Portuguese

your way of listening
serious or laughing, with such patience
during those endless conversations
to practice speaking the language but in the end
really for the pure joy of communicating
your comments suggestions advice
politics history philosophy literature
shared adventures and failures
suffering pain consolation
hopes for the future
your music and poetry
and when I'd leave
your *Até já,*
see you soon,
amigo

About the Author

Hugh Hazelton specializes in the comparison of Canadian and Quebec literatures with those of Latin America. He has published four books of poetry and translates from Spanish, French and Portuguese into English. He is the cohost, with Flavia García, of Lapalabrava, a series of trilingual (French/Spanish/English) poetry readings in Montreal. E.mail: hhazelton@videotron.ca

Adela González-Longoria Escalona

Germination

In the wall,
The old clock,
Accelerates my sunsets;
My hope diminishes
With the trembling shadows.
The earth craves for my body,
Opens to swallow me up
Take me from this mortal confine:
Dust to dust I shall become
The seeds of my love will then be buried
Deep, to germinate again,
Maybe in another spring season.

The Result of Love

My body was fertile ground;
The seeds abundant within my womb,
Time relentless ... many sunsets ...
But the love I nurtured
Has borne the fruit!

Solitude

How can I heal the wounds of my solitude
When without their affliction, I cannot exist …?
I ask you, to reprimand me;
Force my grief down my throat
Often trapped within the silence of the nights.
Return to me: I don´t know
How to live without you, loneliness!

My Search

My dreams are still elusive
Fantasies that have flown away,
But they are out there
Waiting for me somewhere.
The brain is mere flesh:
Dies, its imaginative powers vanish.
But the world around me is a certainty
For as long as it survives in my memories.
Often, I seek unfolding images in empty space
The bitterness of reality, the impossible;
My determined mind bleeds in anguish
And in every drop of my blood
There is the worn out urgency of unachieved dreams.

The Flight of the Word

Don´t let words choke you
by withholding the unwavering truth,
don´t let them hurt you
don´t let them make you profusely bleed;
those who oppress truth abuse you: speak fearlessly
let truth float on the wind, the high seas
resonate up in the mountains,
let it run, diffuse down the roads
echo loud and clear beyond all borders;
let it collide against the rocks and explode
so its phrases turn from mere words
into significant diction to merge and embrace others,
so truth's harmony can freely expand
on its crystal clear transparent wings.

About the Author

Born in 1951 in Gibara, Holguín province, Adela González-Longoria Escalona is member of the Armando Leyva, Espinel Cucalambé and Manuel Gómez Fernández Literary Workshops. She is also member of the Canada Cuba Literary Alliance Sea dreamers of Gibara and is the recipient of various accolades awarded from several literary events, competitions and publications including, The Ambassador, Arrecife and Cacoyuguín newsletters.

Heide Brown

Spring colours

My world
    is constantly re-born
        dressed in more colours
            than I can find
                in my fabrics.

Winter subtleties
    explode into
        an infinite number
             of Spring's extravagant shades.

As a rug-hooker
    how can I
        reproduce my glorious garden
            in all its spring-full glory?

How can
    a studio full of wool
        ever replicate reality?

The Impressionists
    and the Expressionists
        bring me comfort.

Their *creations*
    inspire me
        to *practice my* artistic license
            with my *art*.

The love of my world
    as it dresses for Spring
        is all I need to express.

Chaos

My Aunt Marion said:
Between the stumble and the moving forward is chaos, filled with clues to pathways out.

Her words
    tug at my gut
        tighten my chest
            make my head spin

through the chaos –
      my life appears like a giant roundabout
                          with a thousand possibilities –
      I am dizzy from the many choices.

Maybe this is what chaos is – endless options
  too many
    too *hard*
      to *make choices* …

The clue …
where is *The clue*?

          I never fret …
        never search …
      never even think.
I just breathe and follow my *instinct,*
hoping it will help me find my path …
find the *clues to pathways out* –
      help me to find my way through.

Twenty First Century Tragedy

I'm suffering
    because my little boy is suffering
    my man-child –
        invisibly disabled
            he keeps falling
                through the cracks
                    in the system.

I feel helpless.
    My tears –
        my love –
            aren't enough
                to rescue him.

He lives on the streets
    on a porch
        he states
            describing its comforts:
            cardboard walls
            carpets
            mattress
            bedding.
            All the comforts of home.

Come home!
    I cry.
    He cries too.
        When he occasionally phones.

What can I do?
    Send money, he says.
        Is this the solution
            to his problems?
                The one thing I won't do.
                I won't feed his habit.
                I won't enable his habit.

He has to want real help –
    to take the first steps
        himself.

Meanwhile – I grieve
        for my darling boy.

Lessons from Buddy
(A Eulogy for my Beloved)

Buddy is gone ...
off on his final adventure;
resting with his favourite teddy-friends,
cuddly toys, blankets – in a bed of silk
totally at peace.

My beloved Buddy.
I can still see you ...
your sweet furry face all nestled down and cosy:
I feel if I blink, you will be back
beside me, here on the couch,
thumping your tail and cooing
for more cuddles and more sweet-talk ...
but you've crossed Rainbow Bridge dear Buddy
and my couch will now remain empty and cold.

But I've learned so much from you:
always be curious
breathe deeply
and enjoy each scent
take naps
eat good food
take daily walks, rain or shine
stay comfortable
follow enjoyable habits
always be loyal to those I love
be happy
smile – wag my tail!
patting is good
don't be afraid to leap into the unknown
but watch my feet and
if there's an easier path
make my choice based on my strength
follow my nose

trust my heart
trust my senses
remember being good to others
gets me more treats than growling and snapping
always enjoy my food
ultimately always stay young at heart!

I will never forget your lessons or you
you have been the best teacher I ever had
and I'll never stop loving you ... until we meet again ...

About the Author

Heide Brown started writing when she was 11, producing plays for her Girl Guide friends. Since then, she has filled her file-cabinet with multiple drafts of stories, memoirs and poems, and her bookshelf with journals. Since 1990, she has lived on Gabriola Island, B.C. She loves writing, painting, hooking rag-rugs, her family life, friends, and The Gabriola Commons, which she co-founded. Email: heidebro@telus.net

Joanne Culley

Pioneer in Canadian Entertainment World Brought Joy to Others through Music

As a child I remember my grandmother sitting at the piano and asking me what I would like to hear. I replied: *Tenderly,* my favourite song. She'd start out with flourish, then carry on through, *The Man I Love, Someone to Watch Over Me, Out of Nowhere,* and others from long ago. While Grandma's hands flew across the keys, both she and I would be transported to another time and place – to when she was a star on the radio and stage.

Ida Fernley Culley played piano from when she was about three years old. In 1901, she watched a parade of troops returning from the Boer War, marching to the music, *Soldiers of the King.* When she went back home, she played that song by ear on the piano, note for note. Her parents said she was born with *music in her bones.*

By the time she was seven, Ida was demonstrating new pianos at the Canadian National Exhibition for the R.S. Williams Piano Company. An advertisement said that she was, *the most wonderful child pianist ever heard in Canada,* who had 78 pieces in her repertoire.

Ida was totally focused on her music. While her friends played hopscotch outside at recess, Ida was inside, playing piano for them when they returned to class. She left school after Grade 8 to play accompaniment for the silent movies. That's where she met my grandfather who was also playing piano in a nickel theatre across the street. They married and soon after had two children. Through necessity and her own desires, Ida chose a career path of being a professional pianist, unusual for a woman at that time.

Throughout the 1920s and 1930s, she and my grandfather performed as a duo on the CFRB and CKCL radio stations as the *Black and White Spotters,* as well as playing live on stage at Shea's Theatre, a popular venue in Toronto for vaudeville acts. She took the single stage name of, *Claudette* as she thought it had a more glamorous ring than her given name.

Then the Great Depression came, and the pair lost their jobs as well as their home. But by a stroke of luck, they were seen by Jack Hylton, an English agent and orchestra leader who offered them work overseas.
While touring around the British Isles, Ida and Harry accompanied Bebe Daniels and Ben Lyon, famous Hollywood movie stars who had come to England to perform their musical comedy routine. *The Foursome* was heard all over Europe and England on Radio Luxembourg and they even played at the coronation of King George VI, at the Phoenix Theatre in London in 1937.

My cousin Barbara and I would sit at Grandma's vanity, spraying ourselves with her perfume atomizer, gluing on her false eyelashes and applying her fire engine red lipstick, then we'd pester to see her Norman Hartnell gowns. She'd tell us to get out the old trunk from the hall closet. We'd don the slinky dresses and parade around the room, while she told us that Hartnell was the clothing designer for the Queen.

The entertainers travelled by ship to South Africa to tour the major cities there. When Ida realized that blacks weren't allowed into the theatres where they were performing, she arranged to play special concerts for them, free of charge. But she gratefully accepted bouquets of lilies in return.

Grandma's suede-bound photo album was filled with black and white photos of her in stunning attire, on the ship's deck and in theatre lobbies, along with show playbills and reviews. Even at a young age, I could tell that time was the highlight of her life.

The pair returned in 1938, when rumblings of war were in the air. Newspaper photographs from that time show them modelling the gas masks that had been handed out to British citizens.

By 1939, the Canadian economy was turning around, and they were able to get work on the newly formed CBC radio, on a show called Canadian Cavalcade.

At our annual Christmas Eve family party, Ida would sit down on the piano stool, and would carry on all evening, playing requests from family and friends, amidst lively singing and dancing.

Ida kept up with the times. When Petula Clark's song, *Downtown* became a number one hit in the mid-1960s, she'd listen to it on the radio, then play it by ear with great pizazz to her grandchildren's delight.

As a teenager, I would take her over to the Eglinton Square mall in Toronto. While I shopped for clothes, she'd play piano in the piano store, her songs resonating through the high ceilings. *Demonstrating pianos,* as she had done when she was a child. I must admit, I was a little embarrassed, but everyone seemed to love hearing her music.

In her later years, Ida played for the residents in the Veterans' Wing at Sunnybrook Hospital in Toronto. She was so loved and remembered, that a driver picked her up every week.

We would sit on the verandah, and Grandma would say that she could hear music in the distance, over by Yonge and Eglinton. My cousin Barbara and I would strain our ears, but we couldn't hear anything, just traffic. I think it was a trick of the brain – she was hearing melodies from the past playing in her head in an endless loop.

Ida sat in her chair by the kitchen window and waved at friends and neighbours as they passed by, inviting them in for tea. She'd put out a plate of Peak Freans and regale her visitors with stories of the good old days.

When her health deteriorated to the point where she couldn't live in her own home anymore, I was appointed to help her get ready for the nursing home. When I asked her what she wanted to take, she said mournfully: *How on earth do I know what I'll need there?*

I'm afraid that I didn't know either, but went through her drawers, as I had done as a child, and packed a small bag with her underwear, nylons, slips, night gowns, robe, and a few other articles. I glanced over at the vanity where my cousin and I had preened ourselves, pretending to be her, and thought how beautiful she had once been and still was.

After her death, I gave the eulogy in the packed funeral chapel. I was nervous, as I rarely spoke in public, but I put aside my shyness to pay tribute to a woman ahead of her time, whom I loved and admired greatly. She had found her talent early on and gave it freely to others. She modelled resilience and risk-taking, embracing whatever life threw at her, while forging her own way in the world.

Editor's Note:
UPI Top News reported Ida Culley's death as follows:

March 16, 1983
TORONTO — Ida Culley, a pianist who accompanied many entertainers in the 1930s and 1940s, died Monday in the Cummer Home for the Aged. She was 86.
Mrs. Culley, using the stage name Claudette, and her late husband Harry formed a piano-playing team that accompanied, among others, British comedian George Formby and American singer Kate Smith.
Born in Toronto, Mrs. Culley started playing piano as a child after teaching herself music by ear. At age seven, she was demonstrating pianos at the Canadian National Exhibition.
The Culleys toured South Africa in the 1930s, were featured on Radio Luxembourg and had a half-hour radio program on the BBC after World War II.
The funeral was to be today at Murray Newbigging Funeral Home in Toronto.

About the Author

Joanne Culley received her MA in English Literature from the University of Toronto, and her post-grad certificate in Creative Writing from the Humber School of Creative and Performing Arts. She is an award-winning writer and documentary producer whose work has appeared in the Globe and Mail, Peterborough Examiner, CBC, Bravo Network and more. Email: joanne.culley@sympatico.ca

James Deahl

The Preacher

Spring was set aside for planting in the hill country of Appalachia. Autumn was devoted to the hurried harvest, for frost could arrive early and unexpectedly. No one wanted to be caught with crops in the field when the cold came down from the northlands, for that spelled disaster for a family. And winter . . . Ah, yes winter. From December through March, one would commonly find the narrow hollows choked with snow, for the season fell heavy here.

Summers, then, were reserved for play and revivals. Every sort of minister from the university-educated and properly ordained, to the self-appointed who could scarcely read the Bible would pass through and erect tents, wherever they found people and a level space. In those early days of twentieth-century America, these travelling preachers were as common, and only slightly less annoying, as a plague of locusts.

That summer, my father was an eight year-old lad, and the world was only one short year away from a war, in which his older brothers would serve in the trenches. The hill country was exceptionally replete with evangelists, as though the excessive heat and lack of rain that year summoned them. As a general rule, children had little interest in revival meetings and tedious sermons. The men, often coal miners and railroaders would be tired from their ten and twelve-hour workdays. The women, on the other hand, thought religion was good for the soul, as perhaps it could be – when properly administered. Life was difficult in those isolated communities, especially for married women, and the preachers knew how to elicit their most spiritual feelings.

While the natural beauty of the region was beyond dispute – perhaps without equal in the eastern half of the United States – there was an abiding feeling of loneliness that affected young and old alike. Villages of perhaps only a few hundred people were cut off from each other by poor, or nonexistent, roads. Journeys were often undertaken on horseback. The Appalachians were rugged; their forests dense. And education was generally restricted to one-roomed schools. Most people would live, work, and die within twenty miles of their place of birth. Usually, they married a neighbor whom they had known from childhood. For all the glory, the woodlands of blazing sumac, chinkapin oak, black tupelo, and shagbark hickory, were bestowed on the uplands every autumn. People often longed for another, for a *larger*, life: a life beyond the mountain ramparts. Especially when a chill wind in late October forecast another winter.

A century ago, it was uncommon for villages, like the one my father called home, to provide hotels or inns, or other places of entertainment for travellers. Such few people as passed by, were "put up" in private homes, for the hill country people, although frequently of limited means, were unfailingly generous to sojourners. So, it was that the summer revivalists who journeyed from home to home while spreading the Holy Gospel.

Such a preacher, and one of dubious qualifications, came to my father's village every August as he made his rounds. Father's village was not the finest in the county. Its creek was polluted from the beehive ovens. It flowed orange and black and rancid with acid. The trail shadowing this creek was so obscure that it had escaped the notice of all, but the most obsessive cartographers. This itinerant Gospeller was one of the few to find his way in and out. But find the village he did. Whatever uplifting qualities his sermons might have possessed – my father being too young at the time to judge their theological value – it was an open secret, despite all attempts at discretion, that the preacher found time and energy, when not spreading the good Word, to make the occasional lonely widow happy.

Year after year, life went on with little deviation along the cusp that forever has signalled the northernmost expression of the old southland. Trees were cut, coal was mined, and coke was made. The Baltimore and Ohio Railroad carried it all away to cities, so distant few had ever seen them. Generations passed, but the word of God remained constant. That, and the hard winters. It was one thing to seduce a miner's widow and quite another to "ruin" a young girl, but just such an outrage happened. One year, as the apple blossoms began to fade in early May, a child was born to the sixteen-year-old daughter of a local railroader.

August came around again, and so came the revivalist. Where the toxic creek passed under Route 92, a great chestnut grew, despite the poisoned soil. And this is where the preacher ended his earthly days. His body was left swinging from a branch, as a caution to all who passed as to the wages of sin. Eventually, only a bit of spinal cord and an empty cage of ribs remained, that could not even imprison a crow, as winds roved the length of the hollow through all the seasons of the year.

Previously published in: Iconoclast

Old Orchard
Purdy Country Literary Festival

The water mill's been gone
three generations, perhaps longer,
but the Moira contains its music.
Frogs have taken over the old pond;
Joe-Pye-weed lines the river's banks.
The reading over, the poets disperse –
some to the forest, others walk upstream
in search of the beaver dam.

A few apples ripen on the boughs
of an abandoned orchard,
despite the late spring, the cool summer.
Mahler could have understood
such isolation while nurturing
his bittersweet *9th Symphony*,
a work he would never live to hear,
his health failing, his wife unfaithful.

Mahler finally died never knowing
the great acclaim that was to come.
No one will pick these apples.
They will remain long into November.
If the Moira holds the mill's song,
truly the silent branches of these
enduring trees embody all the grace
of the extended adagio that closes his *9th*.

Previously published in: Umbrel

Japanese Maple
a lament for Raymond Souster

One week before the Day of the Dead
the Japanese maple in my backyard
is almost too perfect, every leaf
incandescent enough to ignite the night,
yet all remain unfallen. You, true master
of the backyard poem, will never see
this tree, nor my wisteria
blown yellow by the winds off Lake Huron.
Nor will we again discuss Robert Lowell
or Kenneth Patchen under your mulberry
during the dog days of a Toronto summer.

*May that day never come when we
finally say goodbye*, you wrote recently.
But that day did come and go a week ago.
In your last backyard poem, you described
leaf-stripped trees facing the bitterness
of winter; today I see my black walnut
retains not one leaf as afternoon
welcomes late October's chill.

Previously published in: Under the Mulberry Tree

Who was Raymond Souster?
Homage to a Great Canadian Poet and Writer

Raymond Holmes Souster, OC was a Canadian poet whose writing career spanned over 70 years: (January 15, 1921 – October 19, 2012). He published over 50 volumes of his own poetry and edited or co-edited several volumes of poetry by others. A resident of Toronto all his life, he was considered as the city's "most loved poet".

"You can't read the history of Canadian poetry without encountering him, yet somehow he remains obscure. His legendary shyness has created, over five decades, a curious form of anonymity: he's at once omnipresent and invisible," wrote Robert Fulford in 1998. He added: "Many of us think of him first as the poet-in-chief of Toronto. Souster is a chronicler of his birth city. A city comes to life only after writers have invented it, and Souster has been among Toronto's inventors, adding a layer of poetic reality to the abstractions of asphalt, glass, and brick. His Toronto poems work like photographs in the Henri Cartier-Bresson tradition, inscribing small pieces of space and time on the memory, catching a moment as it flies."
Born in Toronto, Ontario, Souster grew up in West Toronto near the Humber River. He joined the Canadian Imperial Bank of Commerce at King & Bay Streets in Toronto in 1939 and, apart from four years' service in the Royal Canadian Air Force during World War II, he worked at the bank until retiring in 1984.

Souster was the Canadian poet of his generation most overtly interested in, and influenced by, the contemporary American scene. He was first attracted to Henry Miller, and later entered into lasting friendships and correspondence with Robert Creeley and Cid Corman.

Souster was one of the six founders of the League of Canadian Poets in 1966. He was the League's first president from 1967 to 1972. The early 1960s were a prolific and distinguished period for Souster, culminating in his own Governor General's Award in 1964 for his Collected Poems, The Colour of the Times.

In the late 1960s, he embarked on the revision of his early poetry with a view to its reissue, a project that resulted in a Selected Poems in 1972, and the first four volumes of a now ten-volume Collected Poems in 1980, all of which were published by Oberon Press. Souster has also written fiction under the pseudonyms of "Raymond Holmes" and "John Holmes", for which he has drawn on his Air Force experience

The poet and writer was awarded the Governor General's Award in 1964 for The Colour of the Times; a Centennial Medal in 1967; and Hanging In (1979) earned him the City of Toronto Book Award in 1980.

Souster was named an Officer of the Order of Canada in 1995. The Order of Canada website described him: "One of Canada's most important, widely-read and enduring poets, he has been a vital force for the renewal of poetry since the 1940s. His poems describe life in Toronto, ordinary people and the daily events, feelings and experiences of modern city living. A co-founder of the Canadian League of Poets, he has been a source of encouragement and inspiration to several generations of poets while promoting Canadian literature among students of all ages."

*Souster's Uptown Downtown (2006)
was nominated for the
2007 City of Toronto Book Award.
(Wikipedia)*

Old Woman Bay

Quiero vivir sin verme.
– Federico García Lorca

To live without seeing herself
she became a face on a cliff,
lake water bathing her stone feet.

The scarlet maples are her
unsatisfied passions,
the yellow birches her aging skin.

Northwest winds ruffle
her grey hair;
but when the Hunter's Moon comes

the old woman walks naked
into the bay's still waters,
her flesh young once more.

Her wild hair becomes a raven's wing;
from her body's hidden cave
the green scent of spring,

and the green herons of the bay
sing through her throat
until dawn.

Previously published in: California Quarterly

An Obscure Pleasure

At mid-January
Huron's still unfrozen,
its waters lie steel grey
instead of clear blue.
Ice fishers wait knowing
winter must surely come.

Our mallards long vanished,
geese are found everywhere
refusing to migrate,
as though certain their lake
will maintain the open
waters they need to thrive.

I walk the tip of land
across from the lighthouse
and look at a country
I will visit no more,
where I can never pray
again at my parents' graves.

Like Syrian families
recently resettled
I, too, am exiled.
Whence this obscure pleasure
to realize *this* land
finally has become home?

Previously published in: Tower Poetry

Tundra Swans
for Norma West Linder

Only St. Patrick's Day, more than a month's
serving of winter left, yet they return:
tundra swans soaring up from Delaware's
marshes, the vast reach of Chesapeake Bay.
Under snow-heavy skies, they settle here
on this calm pond east of The Pinery.
Though today they rest on sheltered waters,
the Arctic Archipelago awaits.

How like these swans we seem as we journey
thousands of miles to meet and mate against
all odds; our jubilance lights these cold nights,
warms life's fiercest storms. Desolate forests
stretch farther north than vision goes. After
these birds leave, the sky retains their music.

Previously published in: Philadelphia Poets

About the Author

James Deahl is the author of twenty-seven literary titles, the three most recent being: Red Haws to Light the Field, To be With a Woman, and Landscapes (with Katherine L. Gordon). A cycle of his poems is the focus of the television documentary Under the Watchful Eye. He lives in Sarnia, Ontario. Email: jedeahl@gmail.com

Jorge Alberto Pérez Hernández

Life and Death

A new day sneaks in:
We consciously breathe the air
Feed our bodies,
And idly discover
What lies there at our finger tips.
Human reason slowly progresses
We are body and soul, only body and soul;
The soul leaves the body
Ascends to the sky
The body, what remains rests amidst the fog,
In the dark:
Our lives are but fleeting shadows.

Cloudy and Sunny Days

I walk on earth with a resounding step
On sunny and on cloudy days
Almost speechless.
I sleep endlessly,
Wandering clouds is all I see
A sombre day, like the night
Gloomy skies …
The shackles on my feet suddenly release me,
A dazzling smile comes out of nowhere
That doomsday has not conquered.
When I lift my hands
Like magicians to wave a magic wand
Everything is possible.
I hear a whisper in my ear,
It is my Savior, who never lets me down.

Peace

Time steals my hours
and I seek peace:
I find it among my people, my family,
the waves that break in the endless sea,
on the shores of my town
sings symphonic sonatas
in its depths of coral reefs.
Time crawls on my watch;
yet I am at peace.
I clean my *yola**, row out to sea
and it embraces me
calm today, wild tomorrow;
but still always there for me
and for so many others
who live near it, finding peace
and sustenance letting time pass by:
It seems to wash time away
while we cling on to love and what we have.

*YOLA, is a small boat with no engine or motor. It is a local name, this boat for this type of boat only in Gibara not in other parts of Cuba.

Hope

Sometimes nightmares haunt me
intent on obscuring the life I have;
yet I stand, fight, look up to the sky knowing
I have my Savior, a life ahead, fresh dreams.
Sometimes the days are overcast, I pause.-
They cover me with grey stubborn rain
but I seek shelter, wait, and persevere,
lift my eyes to the heavens in search of consolation
then realize I have a provider,
blessed rain, rainbow bridges
and my eternal relentless hope.

On my way to the water Course

Free Sundays
in the wee hours of the morning
I journey to Montanez watercourse.
I breathe in the pure air
gaze at the weeping forest;
the woods look both happy and ominous.
I see arid crevasses in the distance
and as I approach the watercourse,
I see quivering green carpets everywhere.
Livestock roam idly about
the village, a scene of oak shacks,
no latches in the doors
no boarded windows.
I cross golden rivers
and see peaceful country folk
working from dawn to sunset,
joyous old people
who light their bronze lanterns at night,
joyfully wait for the coming of a new day.

Night in the Sea

When the mysterious night falls
everything stands still,
the ocean dozes off before us
things fade and vanish
creatures sleep ...
Then the gentle breeze,
dawn caresses the quiet waters
ascends slowly, gleefully,-
bringing life to the calm sea
closing the farewell curtains
of the dying night.

The Sea Belongs to us all
To my brother Miguel Olivé

The sea is yours, mine, the wind´s;
It belongs to the poesy that nestles in our chests
That burns in your throat and later dissolves;
That traps and sets you free.
It belongs to those who come and go
To those who feel nostalgic or forget
Those who passed; those newborn babes every day.
It belongs to the curious child who loves his boats
To the tired grandpa who smiles when he remembers,
To the North and to the travelers
To the aliens and emigrants,
To the friends and lovers
To he who inspired me to write these lines:
Because he is my friend and brother
A giant – and a dwarf.
With the capability of being human
And eternally grateful to God;
With an in-built spirit
That fights, never gives up;
His goals clear, his well-chosen profession:
For all that, it also belongs to him, and more,
Because he always loved the sea:
For the huge blue wake that reflects the roof above it.
For its bold yet captivating arrogance.
The sea belongs to me and to those who
Find their livelihood in it.
The sea belongs to you, and to those who ignore it
And fear it but still love it.
For its endless lanes,
For its silent moments and its musicality.
It shrouds, overwhelms other worlds,
Splits fortune among many, unifies dreams.
Unvanquished, piercing, the sea will forever belong
To everyone – and to no one.

Zone 149

There was no hope for the sea to calm down that night. We rowed out on the choppy waves and even the old fishermen could not believe we had decided to dare venture into such strong east winds.

What zone?, asked the dispatcher with a sleepy voice. It was already 12:46 a.m.

Zone 149. We are headed for Punta Rasa, we replied.

It was my first fishing expedition at sea, so the gear was really loaded with fishing lines, hooks, a heavy snack and a brand-new lantern, an unusual object on board. We left in high spirits with rowing vigorously, like two seasoned seamen. Our singing could be overheard, despite the waves' booming sound breaking on the shores. But we did not mind, as we were caught up in the euphoria of the adventure.

Gibara's lights slowly faded in the distance. The wind picked up, but our eagerness to drop our hooks into the water simply overcame the feeling of the risk we were taking.

An hour had ticked away when we discerned Punta Goleta. Then a weak voice reached me, *Do we stay here or move on?*

I insisted, *We move on, man!* Yet something inside me was urging me to return. I felt my Strength starting to diminish as the waves beat against the bow echoing like a drum. As it grew darker, I realized the bottom of the boat was swimming in water. Finally, we made it to Punta Rasa.

Fathom the water and scoop water out of the boat! Jose promptly suggested. He was my first fishing mate.

I took my favorite green fishing line and measured the water depth. *Twelve fathom deep,* I reported.

We dropped the anchor and started our fishing operation. After twenty agitated minutes, my head grew heavy and my sight poor. I was terribly seasick but kept pretending I was fine, so my mate would not realize. Hard as I tried, I came to a point when I was about to lose control so I turned to Jose: *Any bites yet?*

His head was drooping. He was silent and somber. He did not reply. So I rephrased my question: *How are you hanging out in there?*

Suddenly and without warning, he vomited abundantly overboard. That was his answer. I followed next. The wind, the rain, and the inches of rising water inside the boat were increasing. We could no longer remain on our boat bench and chose to lie down at the bottom of the boat both quite aware of the water at the bottom, while the lantern danced to the rhythmic swaying of the sea from prow to stern.

It felt like an eternity later when in the distance I thought I heard the sound of a running motorboat. For an instant I felt great relief. I was so sick, I could hardly raise my head, but with one last superhuman effort, without even looking up to see who or where the sound came from, I picked up the lantern, held it high and shouted: *Mister, Mister! Come and help us, please!*

It was indeed a relief as the sound of the boat came closer and closer. My hope of feeling the steady hard ground beneath my feet again was now a reality. It turned out that our saviours were Pedro, Iván and Fufú, two fishermen friends. They were coming to tow us back to shore. Automatically, but painstakingly, we switched boats. That is how we returned to shore.

That was an awful experience and a terrifying night, but there it is, a deeply rooted memory of my first-time experience as a fisherman.

A Marlin or a Shark – Two Young Men and the Sea

Months after my initiation as a fisherman, my friend Román and I left from our small fishermen's marina berthing place. We motored out from our quiet bay towards the Gulf Stream and further into the northeast. We huddled in our little boat with jackets pulled to our chins as it bobbed up and down on the waves and the south wind blew from behind us. Our ears were buzzing with the roaring of the chugging motor. The night was pitch dark, with phosphorescent water undulating at our gunnels; a night I would have traded for a full moon. We sailed under the veil of darkness, eyes fixed on the black horizon, eager to see the break of day.

At last it was time to fling the boulter. In half-darkness we dropped fishing lines into the abyss and headed further east. This was no easy task, but in our novice's minds' in this trade all was well. With aching hands from the frozen bait, we dropped the sixth line with a *machuelo* that shone like a bobbing pearl. A few minutes later, my mate who was scanning the surface of the sea with eagle eyes yelled: *Estan picando! Están picando! They're biting! They're biting!*

I was a rooky, and didn't know what to say, but I felt butterflies in my stomach as with the inevitable excitement of expectation. Then I heard Román yell the same again. It was dawning and I felt like a seasoned seaman with the vast shoreless sea around me. We continued to throw *lisas* and sardines into the water, while silently praying, with one eye on the sky, there would be no sudden storms. As we dropped the last float, the boulter was pushed by the upstream current. All that was needed now was a keen sailor's eye to spot the fish that would, inevitably, eventually come.

We started the motor, turned the boat and headed for the first set of fishing lines we dropped nearest to the shore. We were anxious to see if the boyhood legends told by old-time fishermen were true. Is it possible that leaping marlin and tuna were capable of sinking ten floats all at the same time, never to be seen again?

We could see the orange markers of the floats in the distance, huddled together, like a row of lined up mandarins waiting for a fight. We moved on to our bobbing fishing lines. Close to the far end, we found scattered floats and started to pull up each drifting line. The first one was light. When we lifted the twenty fathom line, the bait was still intact. We didn't bother to bring up the second line: you could tell by the weight there was nothing. With the third line, Román told me: *There's something! His* hands were shaking. He couldn't even stay on his feet of the swaying boat. *Se ve como un grande, hombre. Looks like a big one, man! Es enorme – It's enormous!* That is all he managed to say as the line was slowly pulled hauled from its black water. I was ready, holding my *mil quince*, my knees firmly set on the right side of *Sabel María*, trying to keep my balance and grabbing the fishing rod to reel in the catch.

Slowly, it came into view. We saw a dark, shadow approaching the surface fast, getting bigger and bigger. We could detect an over three-hundred pound fish, but couldn't figure out what kind. When the fish was in clear sight Román shouted, *Wow, that's helluva marlin!*

I was closer to the prow and could distinguish the first dorsal fin. I shouted, *It's a shark!* Suddenly, the fish swam near the boat. I threw the *mil quince* with all my strength, piercing the tough skin at the back of its head. The mighty fish thrashed in blood spilled water. I gripped the gunnel with white knuckle-terror of falling in. The eye of the fish told me it felt the pain and dived down desperately towards the distant black bottom of the sea. We kept a steady hold, reeling it out a little at a time to wear it out. Our legs were already faltering, but we were certain that the outcome was on our side. As it got closer, we could see the fish had a yellow rope wrapped around its neck.

Roman remarked: *It seems this one has already escaped from another fisherman. I wonder how long it has been swimming with this yellow noose around its neck. It is a shark!*

During the next few flying minutes, we grabbled at the giant fish as it pulled and turned trying to escape. We failed and hit it on the head and the snout. The more we hit it, the angrier it got, until its strength eventually waned and the fish, exhausted, finally relinquished its life to us.

After half an hour of heroic effort the fish was finally quiet and dead.

Román grabbed the tail fin and cut it off with his knife. Pain shot through the fish giving it a second life. It twisted and churned and then with a mighty lunge buried its teeth into the side of the boat. As it spun, the rope was winding around its body like a string on a child's top. We grew more cautious. The enormous fish was repeatedly sticking its head out of the water, looking at us with eyes like daggers. Thank God I never really gave much thought to what would have happened to Román or me, had we fallen into the ocean with him. I only know, the simple terrifying thought of such a scenario makes me shiver to this day.

We tethered the fish from the head and from the tail fin, and reeled it in. The wind was picking up and the boulter was drifting away with the stream. We were tired, but our minds were set on lifting the big catch onto the boat. At the count of three, we pulled the rope together. The boat tilted but we kept at it. The ropes were too stretched already and our hands were numbed and hurting, but we held on and finished our heroic task. The head of the fish now lay beneath the prow, and the tail fin stuck way over the stern. Román and I looked at each other for a few seconds, shook hands and said, *Lo hicimos hermano lo hicimos*! *Brother, we made it, we made it!*

We burst into laughter, drenched in blood and sweat and soaked from head to toe. We gloated over the shark that covered most of the boat, leaving hardly any room for us. There was a mess of ropes and lines that we had to disentangle before reaching the shore …*What do we do now?*

I peeked over my left shoulder and saw a distant orange mark. I said to Román, *Look, the boulter is adrift. Get the oars and out we row*! With all the excitement of our catch, we had forgotten all about the craft of fishing. Fortunately, we reached the boulter and started to bring it up, leaning watchfully over the shark in fear it might still come back to life one last time. We recovered the lines with much effort and exhaustion. We were afraid that another fish might have taken the bait. We had no energy left to fight another fish. Thank God our eyes already perceived the set of fishing lines nearest to the shore, and no other fish was there to fight us.

We spent two endless hours organizing the hooks and the lines. When we finally finished, we put up the sail and started the motor. It was ten past noon when we saw what looked like the, *Silla de Gibara*. We were not really sure, but followed that route until shapes were clearer and we could see the *Punta Rasa* lighthouse.

We felt relieved, yet it would take us hours to enter the base of *Villa Blanca*. It never occurred to me that with a small boat like ours we could sail so many miles and catch such a big fish. On the way back, we killed time planning what we would do and Roman asked: *Are we going to sell it in one piece?*

My mind was blank, but I replied: *I think we should keep something for us*. It was a *Bonitero* shark, and its meat was delicious. Anyway, it was a long stretch before reaching the shore. We could hardly move and were afraid because the sea was choppy and water splashed against the sides, swamping the gunnels. Our thoughts were in turmoil: it was crazy to carry a shark like that on a small motor boat in rough seas.

Well, Román and I had already jumped the gun – I mean, the boat and decided we would finish the job safely, so we did. We arrived at the fishing base after six. The base was swarming with fishermen of all ages impressed with our catch. Eight of them helped us carry the shark from the boat onto dry land.

That day I reveled in pride thinking, I was a great fisherman – instead of a marlin we had caught a great big shark.

*Translation and revision of both stories
by Miguel Angel Olivé Iglesias*

About the Author

*Jorge Alberto Pérez Hernández, Canada Cuba Literary Alliance (CCLA) Ambassador in Gibara, Cuba. He has a Bachelor's Degree in Education, English Major and published stories in Spanish and English for the CCLA. Jorge edited his own work including three books and publications in CCLA's newsletter, The Envoy. He writes mostly about the sea, God, events in life and his family. He loves fishing and runs a home-based B&B.
Email: jorgealbertoph@infomed.sld.cu*

Keith Inman

A Place to be from

Why would you want that
in the living room? she asked

pointing to a picture of a bare
wooden house
with dish cloth curtains
a front door missing trim

and a single power-wire
up the boards and across the sky
out of range of the camera

no eaves channeled rain
to fieldstone gardens dressed
with tall blades of grass
and a few straggled vegetables
crowded by a one-step stoop

a cane chair in the yard sat empty
beside dark-haired, wind-rumpled children
in cotton print cloth standing unsure
of what a photograph was

I asked where she thought
this house was?
Looks kind a like
a place I stayed at in Cuba
with singing geckoes
under that moon
of theirs.

This was my mother's house, I said,
in Niagara. The place I'm from.

Light of the Ocean

Three coves along the coast and the motor
snorted to a stop, a burro refusing to move.
Carlo huffed and puffed against the rewind
of the cord, but she wouldn't go.

Tino worked the oars toward the narrow
of the islands. The boat reeling in passage,
as his matchstick arms fought the turn of tide.

Together, they couldn't have lit more fire
under the sinking darkness than the line of sun
drawing down behind them as shadows took shape,
a hut, a boat, high among the scrub.

Tino jumped out and ran the shore to the bare
wooden door. The knock echoed under tin.

A boat lay strewn with old nets, broken gear
and a few pop cans. A clean motor on the transom.

They carried the engine to their boat and were soon
puttering home. Carlo thinking, he knew
who the owner was, but told himself a storm
could rise any moment, and he worried himself home.

A week later, looking for extra petrol, Carlo
stood outside the Liberato explaining, carefully,
the meat of his story to Juan de Jesus himself,
Juan's scarred cheek twitching to music Carlo

couldn't hear. Juan spat on the ground.
I just fix that thing. She run good, eh?
Thank you my friend for when you bring her back.
And he limped the thirty kilometres home.

Howl

Roosters woke him before the alarm.
Their short 'er-ers' curling into a long drawl
that echoed from the far side of camp
and through the thatch roof.
He keyed the phone and laid back.
The chickens had claimed the day, and could now
eat, shit and be happy.

The bar fridge cycled up.
Its cold core cooling the main chamber
as Tocororo's across the lagoon
began cooing for partners.
He rolled over and buried his head
under the covers. Her breast was soft
on his cheek, like the low rumble of her
breath. Her nipple hardened into his eye.
Come on. Get up, he said.

Her bronchia fired up the moment she opened
her eyes, a spurious hack
of chunks rattling from the lungs. Smokers cough,
the doctor had said. Though, she'd never
smoked. Wasn't even fifty?

They dressed slowly for the bird walk at six.
A final adventure before an overnight flight
back to winter-land. He thought
the humidity here would have done more.
Maybe, they needed to move here. Sell the house.
Cars. RRSP's. The dog. The kids. Their Future
for a future. He held the flashlight for her
and turned off the porch bulb. His offered hand
down the rough sawn planks to the stone path
was pushed aside. *I'm not helpless,* she said
sidestepping into the weakened darkness.

In the middle of nowhere, he turned back
to shut the door.

Belly of the Whale

I un-shutter an eye
of this old
Hemingway Hotel
to see what jazz
splashes below
in cobbled streets
worn smooth
by salt tears

a school of tourists
pool in the shallows

reveling
away from sharks and rays
of home

incessant with life
their warm thrashing voices echo
through the hollow
bricks of these Jonah walls

the cracked-rib façade
spewing rebellion
over tiled roofs

an echo washing down
to the shushing sea.

Four Degrees of Light

Sheets of lead darkness wrap
journey's legs. Awake
she lies within a wall of shadow
rimmed with morning.

A soft wind pulls the curtains
closed. The book she's been reading
is on the floor, page open
to everything. In the corner

responsibility, dressed in work,
straps on a watch, twists
a ring on his finger and pads
down a hall of indifference.

Sugar and starch are wrestled
into knapsacks of collecting,
threads without end, and are hurried
onto a bus to rush to whomever

they might become, while wonder
clasps tight to the bedrail and wails
into the dizzying height of breath.

From SEAsia, Black Moss Press, Canada, 2017

About the Author

Keith Inman was a factory worker. His poetry has been compared to Atwood, Boyden and Itani (Canlit 223). A new book, SEAsia from Black Moss, sets binary forces of place, character and circumstance against each other, as Death watches from a hedgerow. Home is the inland port of Thorold, Ontario, where huge ships climb the continent. Email: inman@vaxxine.com

Norma West Linder

Laughing Matters

Ellen Donovan sat on the edge of her daughter's bed, fingering the handmade butterfly quilt. She had run out of arguments against the coming marriage. She repeated her question: *Do you really want to spend your life with a man who despises the way you laugh?*

Cindy lifted a tear-stained face. *I love him, Mom. I get weak in the knees when he kisses me. Actually weak in the knees! And he wants to marry me before we sleep together. How many boys in this town would be like that? He's special.*

Lorne's photo on Cindy's bedside table seemed to be looking at Ellen with disdain. She had to admit – he was handsome, with his thick curls of black hair and deep-set blue eyes. Much too serious looking though for a twenty-one year old. No trace of a smile. He was so quiet around her – acted as though he knew she was against his engagement with Cindy and their upcoming nuptials.

Won't you give us your blessing ... please?

Ellen gave a resigned sigh: *I suppose I might as well. Been trying to change your mind for days now without success.*

Thanks, Mom. I wouldn't want to have to go ahead without it.

Ellen lifted a corner of the quilt – a bright blue butterfly. *Your grandma made this quilt before she married your grandpa. You inherited your great laugh from her. I'm reminded of Mom's laugh whenever I hear yours.*

I wish she and Gramps could be here for my wedding. And Dad too, of course. If only he hadn't gone on that fishing trip ... I always dreamed he'd walk me down the aisle. Storms can come up so suddenly on the Great Lakes ... without warning ...

They fell silent for long moments.

Finally, her mother spoke: *I know, Cindy. Now it's just us two. We mustn't ever let anything come between us. I wish I could afford to give you the wedding you deserve. But I'm afraid we'll have to keep the guest list short – and have the reception right here at home.*

That's okay, Mom. Our house is plenty big enough. And Lorne doesn't have that many friends.

Understandable, thought Ellen. But she was determined to keep smiling. *We'll have lots of champagne* she went on, *and I know a good caterer who'll supply the cake and food. I'll even buy you that white satin gown in Taylors' window – the strapless one you've had your eye on.*

Cindy reached out to hug her mother. *You're the best mom in the world!*

Contrary to what you claimed earlier, I just want you to be happy. Now we'd both better get some sleep. It's almost two o'clock, and we'll have a busy day tomorrow.

Still filled with misgivings, Ellen planted a kiss on her daughter's forehead and left, closing the door quietly behind her. Cindy had always been a wilful girl. At nineteen, she still was. Once her mind was made up, there was no changing it. But at least, she intended to go ahead with her education, aiming for a degree, so she could become a social worker. Maybe that was behind her decision to start dating Lorne, Ellen decided. He was so uptight. Didn't seem to know how to relax and just have fun. He'd even talked Cindy out of having an engagement ring, saying he would buy her a diamond on their first anniversary.

A mechanic in his father's garage, Cindy had met Lorne when she'd taken the car in for an oil change. They'd been dating for the past few months, and Ellen had hoped Cindy would tire of being with such a joyless companion. That hadn't happened, and now her worst fear was coming to reality. It was four in the morning before she managed to drift into a troubled sleep.

* * *

The Big Day had arrived. Everything was ready. It was the fifteenth of June and the sun was shining. Cindy stood in her mother's bedroom, while Kate, her Maid-of-Honour, put the finishing touches on her best friend's upswept chestnut-coloured hairdo.

You look fabulous! she exclaimed.

Ellen agreed, but she saw a troubled expression in her daughter's brown eyes, eyes so much like her own. *Kate,* she says, *could you leave us for a few minutes?*

Sure thing. Mother and daughter time. She left, closing the door gently behind her.

I know something's wrong, Cindy. Talk to me. It's not too late to change your mind you know.

But Mom, all the preparations you've made ... the food ... the flowers ...

Forget that. Just tell me why you're looking so miserable on what's supposed to be the happiest day of a girl's life.

Oh, Mom, I've made a terrible mistake. I must have let my weak knees make me weak in the head.

Ellen resisted the urge to say, *I told you so. What made you see the light?*

Yesterday Lorne and I went to that comedy that's being staged here – the one called, 'Fringe Benefits'. It was hilarious. I started laughing too loud and he put his hand over my mouth. He actually clapped his hand over my mouth! I was so stunned I just sat there. But I can't stop thinking about it.

Nor should you, Cindy. That's a red flag if ever there was one. Did I ever tell you that Dad fell in love with Mom the first time he heard her big hearty laugh? He was passing the door of the yoga class she was instructing, and one of her students had told a funny story about a guru. He loved the sound of that laugh! My parents were able to celebrate their Golden Wedding Anniversary, something that's becoming a rare event in today's world. I'm pretty sure you and Lorne wouldn't make it to the first one.

But all the expense you've gone to …

Hang the expense. I'll ask Kate to go to the church and tell Lorne you've changed your mind. That you're far too young to marry. Kate's a strong person. She can handle it. With that, Ellen summoned the girl.

After explaining the situation, Ellen asked, *Can you do it?*

Gladly, Kate replied.

Ellen Thought, that single word speaks volumes. She has not been the only one to have misgivings. *Tell everyone the reception's still on. There'll be lots of food and champagne. And their gifts will be returned.*

I'll drink to that, says Kate as she takes her leave.

Ellen turned to her daughter. *Put that gown back into the box it came in. Save it for the right man – and the right time.*

Cindy hugs her and laughs with relief. *You really are the best mom in the world!*

Choices

On a sudden whim, Nuala decided to spend her holidays visiting Ireland to search out the burial place of her father's family, the Foleys of Cobh.

One presence in particular haunted her – her dad's only sibling, Bridie. A woman whose likeness she'd studied years earlier in a dog-eared family album. Though she'd been just a youngster of ten at the time, she'd been able to see a resemblance between herself and her aunt destined to remain forever a stranger to her. They had the same thick auburn hair and dark blue deep-set eyes that seemed too intense for the rest of their faces. It was a shame her dad wasn't well enough to travel with her.

Poor Aunt Bridie. Dead at nineteen. She and her infant buried in the same coffin.

Her father hadn't told her that, until she was a teenager. It had made a tremendous impact on her. She'd taken out the album many times to stare for long minutes at snapshots of the solemn looking young woman. In one of them, Bridie was standing at the base of a hill, wooden houses inclining sharply upwards behind her. She was wearing some sort of smock. Perhaps she was pregnant then. Her dad had told her, Bridie had died during childbirth in 1949, after naming her child, Nuala. Grief-crazed, her husband had taken off to an unknown destination. Nobody in the family heard from him ever again. It was rumored he'd gone to Australia.

The sun was shining when Nuala left Dublin to travel by train to the little island of Cobh, where the old cemetery at Ballymore was located. It was a bank holiday and the old harbour town of Cobh looked deserted, though now and then she fancied, she could see faces peering from behind white lace curtains. The feeling seemed particularly strong when she paused on what might have been the very spot where Bridie had posed in her maternity smock back in the forties. She hurried on under an August sky that was rapidly becoming overcast. She turned as a middle-aged woman in black came striding up the hill towards her. *Excuse me,* she began, *could you direct me to the Ballymore Cemetery?*

Tis far from here, the woman replied without slowing her pace, or looking back.

Nuala shivered as her only human contact disappeared over the crest of the hill.

She glanced back towards the water at the imposing church, its spires rising like a cluster of granite spears against the pewter-coloured sky. She thought a priest would probably be able to tell her where her aunt lay buried.

The guilt she thought she'd finally exorcised months earlier hit her the moment she entered Saint Colman's Cathedral. Almost of its own volition, her hand was making the age-old sign of the cross. She sank to her knees. *Mea culpa, mea maxima culpa,* she murmured. She heard again Ron's anguished voice, *Don't go through with this, please. Everything will work out. You'll see.*

But she'd had the abortion anyway. One year ago. And she hadn't seen Ron since then. Nor had she wanted to. What he'd done was unforgivable.

After a time, Nuala rose. Put it behind you, she told herself. Ron hadn't been honest with her. Anyway, she was young and she had her career in advertising to think about. There'd be time for babies later. The thing to do now was find a priest and get the information she needed.

Nuala pounded in vain on the door of the first rectory in a line of rectories. At the third knock, a disgruntled housekeeper cracked opened the door a crack. *Ye'll not find anyone today,* she replied in answer to Nuala's request. *Come back when it's not a holiday.*

With that, the door was slammed unceremoniously in her face. Then she retraced her steps back up the hill. All six thousand residents of Cobh, she decided, must have taken advantage of the bank holiday. It took her half an hour to find a taxi. Rain began to fall. The driver looked surprised when she told him her destination. *Not the best weather to go there,* he said.

Fortunately, the shower stopped just as they reached the wild, forlorn cemetery. *I'll probably never be able to find my aunt's stone*, Nuala confessed as the cabbie opened the door for her. *But I'd like to be alone to look for it. Could you come back in an hour?*

No trouble, Missus. But I can help you. Me own mother's buried right near your Foleys. I'll show you the spot, so.

Together they stumbled through the long grass and over the bumpy terrain dotted with Celtic crosses of all sizes. Nuala thought she'd never seen a more desolate place.

Watch yer step, Missus, the driver cautioned. *There's holes in here deep enough to break a leg.*

On the grave of the cabbie's mother, she noted a clear plastic bell filled with red roses. He stooped to brush away a pile of dead leaves before departing.

Nuala scarcely noticed him leave, so lost was she in studying the stone slab at the end of a mound of long yellow grass. DIED, AUGUST 8th, 1949. August the eighth – the very date she'd checked into the hospital for the abortion. An icy feeling caused the fine hair on her bare arms to rise. She pulled on the green sweater-coat she'd been carrying and hugged herself to stop trembling.

She wished again, as she'd wished so often, that she'd never been told the fetus was female. The nurse had been severely reprimanded for her breach of confidence, but that hadn't helped Nuala when the bad times came. She thought she'd gotten all the anguish out of her system. The grave before her looked like the last resting place of the loneliest of the lonely. Not like her mother's, back in Canada. No husband to put flowers here – not even plastic roses.

Nuala backed off and sat on a rock half hidden in tall grasses. She pulled a pack of cigarettes from her bag. She'd been trying to quit, but she needed one now. She kept picturing Bridie and the infant daughter she was named after, in a forever embrace in one coffin. Right here, under the ground, not far from her feet. Her hands were shaking so badly, she gave up trying to light the cigarette and sat with it clamped in her mouth. The cemetery was horribly quiet. No song of bird to break the stillness. It was growing dark too quickly. A wind was rising, stirring the rain-dampened trees behind her. It had been a mistake to send the cab driver away. She wanted to be anyplace but here.

Nuala flung the cigarette away. What was she doing perched on a barren rock in this centuries old cemetery … in this wilderness of tilted tombstones? She must have been crazy to come alone to this God-forsaken spot, letting ghosts of the past get to her.

The wind was rapidly becoming a gale, bearing with it the pungent smell of the nearby Atlantic. *Bridie,* she whispered, *oh, Bridie.*

All at once, a small animal scuttled across Nuala's sandaled feet. She screamed and jumped up, dropping her bag as she ran forward. Her right foot caught on something hard and she fell headlong, badly twisting her ankle. For a nightmarish moment, she awaited the cabbie's return, calling out sporadically, frightened by the sound of her own voice. When finally he came, he had to help her every step of the way back to the taxi.

He took her straight to his own doctor in Cork. *You'll like Dr. Brian Davies,* he promised her. *He's a kind man, so. And tonight you can stay with me and me wife. We run a Bed and Breakfast called Molly's, after herself. Only fair since she does all the cooking.*

She did like Dr. Davies. Liked him so much, she found herself spilling out her life story as he bandaged her sprained ankle, relieved when he assured her there was no real damage.

Doctor, what is your opinion of a man who would lie about a vasectomy, so he could get a woman pregnant and trick her into marriage?

He must have wanted so much to keep you. I'm almost sorry for him. But what he did was wrong.

What I did was wrong too. I know that now. But how could I marry a man I didn't love? In the beginning, I thought I did. Then, I realized we weren't right for each other. I couldn't go on with the pregnancy, couldn't face raising a child on my own. They're right when they say that guilt is the gift that keeps on giving. I can't seem to shake it off.

Miss Foley, Nuala, you have to put the past where it belongs. In the past. We all make choices in life, and then we have to move forward.

I'm so sorry for babbling on like this. I don't know what got into me. I guess the business about the date on Bridie's tombstone took on significance out of all proportion. Look at me! I'm a mess. I can't stop trembling.

You should go back there – to Ballymore. Get back on the horse, so to speak.

What? Oh, no. I couldn't.

That's exactly why you should. My wife and I will go with you if you like.

You'd do that for me? A stranger?

You seem to me a stranger who needs a friend. Besides, my wife's grandfather is buried in a cemetery near there. He was on the Lusitania when the Germans sank it early in the WWI. We'll take a lunch and make a day of it.

That's so good of you, doctor. Your middle name must be kindness.

Actually, it's Boru. I'm named after Brian Boru, the High King of Ireland, back in one thousand and something. My mother was a bit of a romantic.

I suppose my mother was, too. Naming me Nuala after a lost infant.

Well then, we have something in common. We'll pick you up from Molly's on Sunday and we can all go to Ballymore together.

Together, thought Nuala. The word had a comforting sound.

Author's Bio

Member of The Writers Union of Canada, Norma West Linder is a novelist, poet, and short story writer. She lives in Sarnia, where for 24 years, she taught English at Lambton College. Her latest publications are: The Pastel Planet, a children's novel; Tall Stuff for adults, and Two Paths through the Seasons, a poetry collection with James Deahl. Email: nlinder@cogeco.ca

James Cockcroft

Lying in bed I reached over

Lying in bed,
I reached over,
not taking you in my arms
as I sometimes do,
nor you me.

Not cuddling,
though often
we do.

I slipped my arm
behind your neck,
and your shoulder,
hunched my fingers
as my other hand
found your arched hip,
and our toes met.

A kind of current
coursed from those
points of contact,
not as strong as
electricity, nor
as weak as
thin water flow,
but all through me.

Back to you,
back to me,
with not one
of us left alone,
joined by the
arc ...

Did you feel it too,
a sinuous charge
from somewhere inside
each of us?

I gave in to
it, wondering
would it stop,
continue,
intensify,
fade?

I told you of it and,
dull with sleep,
you replied:
Uh-huh.

It continued
flooding back and forth
through its circuit,
unaffected
by our words.

I said to you,
not loud enough,
to wake you:
I will write a poem …

About the Author

James Cockcroft is a bilingual award-winning author of 50 books, including, Why? Por Que? Pourquoi? Poetry & Poesia published by Hidden Brook Press, 2009, 2nd ed. 2013, Canada and Mexico's Revolution Then and Now, NY: Monthly Review Press, 2010, now in 5 editions and 3 languages. Email: jcockcro@yahoo.com

Manuel García Verdecia

Beatles' blues

past yeah the dream's already passed
it's too much dust more than twenty years
we're walking along a nightmare
the dream's just memory friend memory
we used to have long hair
an endless wish like the long hair
we gave one another rain and early mornings
the sun playing in seventh chord
was telling us time never waits
nothing waits for us nobody waits for us
we slept little avoiding to play death
there isn't any time friend but today
a guitar and a girl as real as her eyes and her legs
it's too much dust more than twenty years
nights, we gathered like stars
in *Lucy's sky with diamonds*
to listen to the good old records
with the new gospel in the electric voices
of John Paul George and Ringo
oh yeah how close the world was then
the whole world fits in a girl and a song
Michelle, ma belle…
every girl was her
I need you, I need you, I need you
you'll never be Eleanor Rigby
picking up the rice of someone else's wedding
we promised each other the most faithful rice
look at all the lonely people
also look at the blind ones
who don't believe in songs flowers or sex
but in something very serious and big
like god's never seen face
yeah we had a cause friend

*sergeant Pepper's lonely hearts club ban*d
and we longed for a marmalade sky
one we could grab and eat
help listen dear old ones *help*
let us do it our way as we can *help*
a simple sky in pop-art colors
and a peace-and-love symbol shining high ...
but all that is just past friend
it's much dust more than twenty years
now everything is less
death deletes chunks of memory
loneliness howls at every corner
dreams are all in tatters and *they*
are just a shadow that moans in the air.

Birds
(For my friends)

Here in my yard birds always come
To break the day
Then divide the hours.
They come and go because there are no barriers,
No one requests signatures or documents
Most times they do not return here:
Though perhaps some good neighbor
Is repeatedly gratified for the view whenever they do.
It is important we understand
Without interceding rituals or promises
That when nothing is asked no one bothers.
Here they find bread, home, a little water,
They rest, sing, eat and meet.
The celebration of life is joy
An offering to anyone who believes:
I see they are not frightened away
Some of them stay with me,
Some part of me will always
Go with them there;
Though they'll never know what hand
Provides each day the bread and water.

On the Human Lament

(Aaah! we shall never know how to fight against this cry
echoing within ourselves – Ceslaw Milosz)

And what is that cry, is it the uproar of grief,
the noise of anxiety breaking down,
of bones breaking, the green wood of life in flames
us that cannot stand anymore our sobbing,
or does it all come from others, the list of all those blunders,   nightmares and fears,
a river that goes through our heart carrying the murmur of so much
                                                            rebellious blood?
Destiny grinds dreams, longings, wishes
and makes resounding thunder not allowing us to look serenely at the
                                      dawn, or feel the smoothness of air;
the cry is an attempt to entice life, a tremor of sense, wishing to find
                                                          its place.
Existence is like a mule that can no longer bear its burden and
                                        succumbs or collapses,
then it brays in distress –
everything begins with a cry
storm – crash of lightning the effort of a woman in labor, the wonder of the
       a newborn, the repentance of the condemned man, the
          conscience of the executioner, the fatigue of the moribund –
             the collapse of the depressed, the sighing of the
                one that doesn't want to live any longer, the vacuum of the one that
                cannot find death ...
This succession of miseries and resignations, this covetous
       accumulation of hours vegetative days and months,
this constant clamor bursting out, the rush that
     gathers and smothers could be understood without the relief of
     that tormented water.
We cannot silence the claim of our longings, the protests of our sorrows,
          the wailing of our vulnerability;
the cry is a monotonic and out-of-tune hymn
but a sign that life still sends
hope a desperate token that launches
the lament, a spell to redeem us from this horror ...

The Wall
(Bodhidharma spent nine years staring at a wall until he attained illumination)

a maniac's bald head with hawk eyes
a faded raven of sparse dull plumage staring
with a drunkard's anguish
an odalisque who gives away her turbulent rump
a ship with shabby folded sails
a legendary ghost ship on an icy sea
a bishop with open arms
pacifying the multitude

a mad fate has tied me relentlessly
a whole life of agony before this wall
I interrogator of so many impulses
try to find the revealing light
but I'm always defeated by the visions
on this wall that were given to me
so dark so coarse so elusive

About the Author

Former associate professor of the Teacher Training College of Holguín, Manuel García Verdecia is a poet, writer and translator. He has worked for the Cuban Organization of Writers and Artists and is visiting professor at the Teacher Education English Major Department at Holguín University, at the Shakespeare Studies Centre and the Canada Cuba Literary Alliance.

Photograph by Shane Joseph

Photograph by Wency – Wenceslao Alexander Rosales

Photograph by John Hamley

Photograph by Richard M. Grove

Lisa Makarchuk

The Age of Trump – September 11, 2017

The Dark Ages are upon us again
Forces of ignorance on the ascent,
Smothering fires of creativity
Darkening them in their descent,
Destroying reason and rational thought
Replacing these with hatred and lies;
Increasing corruption, spreading its rot
Furthering suspicion, hypocrisy,
Stalking our neighbour, blotting the light
Kept at bay only by an active foresight,

Seize back those fires of imagination, conciliation,
Negotiation and tolerance – enough of their lies
These new embers we light; bringing them to life
Feed that fire; dispersing its might,
By flooding Trump's ignorance with our insight.

So burn, burn, ye fires of science
And of sane and sensible thought;
Fan your sacred flames higher
Burn to set your conscience ablaze
Burn without stop; undo this craze,
Burn to overcome what keeps us in thrall,
Burn to bring back some brilliance
Burn in order to save us all.

Rape of Nanking
(The Other Holocaust – December 13, 1937)

fascist troops entered Nanking and
seven weeks of killing ensued
unleashing rape, atrocity,
and with hatred imbued
killing hundreds of thousands,
their bodies were strewed
through city streets
befouled, eviscerated,
disemboweled, bayoneted:
breasts were sliced off
women defiled then nailed alive
to walls, naked ones made to sit
on hot charcoal stoves
continuously lit;
civilians were tied unto trees
kicked to death, and babies
sliced in half, thirds and quarters
people subjected to electric tortures
kerosene pumped through hoses
forcibly placed into mouths and noses
rupturing bowels excreting their swill:

in parts of the city
people were suspended
until they would feel
their bodies distended
children screaming, weeping
from medical experiments;
people alive but half-buried
German shepherds ferocious
and scary, tearing
their innards apart:

evil harvested the city; it came
in the grotesqueness of
frenzied soldiery who claimed
a superior race mentality
sharing convenient indifference
and studied acceptance
by those exercising no resistance
to this genocidal existence:
what is it in war and battle that happens?
soldiers' morality subsumed under flame
we've heard it over and over: NEVER AGAIN.

On Alert for Democracy

Democracy
elusive in its concepts
Thomas Paine's *"Rights of Man"*
fertilizing its depths
reaching for new aspirations
greening from budding inspirations.

But what is its meaning today?
Optimism has withered
on futile hopes in midst of decay
a rudderless ship just barely floating,
grounded on deep shoals of violence
division, despair.
Was it meant to mean police brutality
a flouting of lawful stability,
a furthering gap between rich and poor
race wars, a dying planet,
inescapable hatred and unceasing wars?

Our young people die in faraway places;
it is said to defend our democracy
but who threatens it?
No Iraqi ever bombed my home
no Afghani tortured people I know,
no Salvadoran exploited my resources,
no Vietnamese ever poisoned my crops,
no Libyan forces determined my fate
by turning my country
into a lawless state.

Is it democracy where groups gain control
of a Congress that can be bought and sold,
lobbyists bestriding its halls
elected officials by money cajoled
the planet's imperiled
by a system that's rotted?
A new world is needed it seems
a yearning return
to Thomas Paine's dreams.

About the Author

Lisa Makarchuk is Co-ordinator of the first International Festival of Poetry of Resistance. She wrote copy for radio, news articles and published essays in Cuba Solidarity in Canada. She edited IFPOR Anthology 2011, Vol.1, published poetry in Crossing Borders, Resistance Poetry 2, and In Bottom of the Wine Jar. An associate member of the League of Canadian Poets, she is vice-president of the Canada Cuba Literary Alliance.
Email: lisamakarchuk@sympatico.ca

Mary Lee Bragg

Two Resorts

On a boulder on the beach at Guardalavaca
Christopher Columbus left his feet
when his statue toppled and flew east
during the last hurricane.

The sign *Hotel – tlantico*
overlooks the bare rock,
a giant *A* soaring after Columbus.

Each day a maid changes
our transparent sheets,
folds threadbare towels
into swans or hearts,
decorated with hibiscus flowers
that make us sneeze.

Canadians sing of ice and snow,
and swim up to the bar
for Pina coladas.
One dons snorkel gear
to splash in the fountain.

Quiet in our room,
we surf the TV channels:
Chinese agricultural report
weather in German,
Trailer Park Boys
BBC News.

Farther down the beach
at Guantanamo,
another Canadian would like to hang
the *Por favor, no moleste* sign
on his door.

Eight years Khadr breathed sea air,
watched palm trees flaunt beyond the fence,
contemplated stars and moon
embedded in a sky
so dark and clear,
a true sailor
could navigate by night.

Previously published: Award-winning chapbook,
Winter Music Tree Press, Canada, 2013

Living in Public

The *Caballero de Paris* walked the streets of old Havana in his cape and high boots, hands full of books, his matted hair and beard unfurling behind him.

He was rich in Paris, he said, a nobleman. *Habañeros* fed him, charity for the mad, for his craziness bred in prison on a false charge.

Today he strides in bronze down the sidewalk in front of the bookstore bearing his name. His metal beard shines, polished by hands touching it for luck.

We are not so lucky. Our guide tells his story and we look at the statue from a distance.

A girl in ball gown and tiara poses for a professional beside, before, behind the *Caballero*. It is her *Quinceañera* and her hips are swaying with the excitement of being this day's queen.

In the hotel elevator that night we step between two people. She is red-faced and tear-streaked, he is clenched in the opposite corner. In the French of *Ste-Foy* between four and lobby, she tells him: *J'ai eu des malheurs avec toi.* I've been miserable with you.

We stare at the ceiling, pretend we don't understand, though the universal language of the body tells all.

How much of my life is instantly visible? Servers and beggars speak to me in English, speak in front of me as if I couldn't possibly understand French, or Spanish. From the soles of my *Teva* sandals to the crown of my Tilley hat, I exude the smell of money, a *norte Americana* who doesn't need to touch the *Caballero*'s beard to have four *Quinceañeras* of good luck.

I hold my husband's hand as we walk through the lobby. *Let's never do that. Not in the elevator*, he agrees.

Previously published: Windsor Review in 2016,
and long-listed in Best Canadian Poems, 2016

Lisbon

In Lisbon, we climb.

By day, narrow sidewalks
and steep streets,
dodging dog dirt on cobblestones
in Alfama, Graca and Barrio Alto.

We climb winding staircases
to the top of the tower of Belem
and the basilica of Estrela
the star.

We take the public escalator up six flights,
emerge in front of the pastry shop
where the poet Pessoa and friends
debated art.

In bronze he sits outside,
knees and hand polished
by visitors perching
for photos.

My muscles hold the memory.
Like a dog twitching after rabbits
in its sleep
I climb all night.

In dreams
I shinny up a steeple
and grapple with a
thousand rungs of ladder.

At the top
Pessoa's shining hand
reaches for mine
and helps me up.

Previously published: Award-winning chapbook,
Winter Music Tree Press, Canada, 2013

Rossio

The German businessmen did not set out to be part of history.
They are, by definition, minding their own business.
They represent the family firm, which specializes
 In finely-milled precision instruments of death.

They wear spats and gaiters and detachable celluloid collars
with hooks and buttons in many under-layers of clothing.
They think they are up to the minute, but the minute is 1910.

It's a moment in history like1999 that will soon be so eclipsed
by what came after that we wonder if we imagined it.

Portugal in October is too warm for woolens.
One of the Germans wipes his face with a large white handkerchief.
This businessman often daydreams that a beautiful woman
is crying in his arms and he holds the handkerchief to her face,
while pressing her to his manly breast. In this daydream,
bosoms and chests are more prominent than noses.

None of the Germans have a cell phone or laptop
and no one texts to tell them Rossio train station
in Lisbon is under siege. It's a revolution,
and the city is all cobblestones at the barricades.

When the train pulls into the station finely-milled instruments
of death are pointed through the windows at them.
The businessmen are marched along the platform
down a long staircase to where daylight
streams through doors like inverted horse-shoes.

Outside those doors is a city with hotels and meeting rooms,
offices and warehouses. And now the romantic
waving his handkerchief for safe passage enters history.

He does not emerge into confusion. He creates it.
What does a white flag mean, but surrender?
The besieging crowds erupt in cheers so loud
that the last royalists know the war is over.
They come out with hands up behind the travellers
who have already gone to their hotel to bathe.

For four years, the revolution in Portugal
is the businessman's most exciting story.
Then his life becomes much more exciting,
and then it is over.

Previously published: Award-winning chapbook,
Winter Music Tree Press, Cana

About the Author

Mary Lee Bragg's poetry and short fiction have appeared in literary magazines and e-zines in Canada, the USA and Cuba, including, Ascent, Bywords Quarterly, CV2, Queens Quarterly and the Windsor Review. She published two poetry chapbooks: How Women Work (2010) and Winter Music (2013). She lives in Ottawa. Email: mlbragg@sympatico.ca

Richard Marvin Grove (Tai)

My Light Blinks Off
Thank you Lillian Allen

Sometimes I feel like it is a dreary life.
Me squinting at my florescent light-beamed desk
facing a concrete, windowless wall
day after day, after day. My plywood bench
scattered with screws, tools, a mother board leans
against the wall lifeless waiting to be installed.

A screw plinks to the floor; I come to life, screech
my stool to the side to reach, I flinch, I bend,
I stretch and squint to look. The screw has disappeared.
While I am on my knees groping, searching, I wonder why.

Before me, my father was a small appliance technician. Why
on earth did I follow in his steps, stooped in a viewless,
stuffy room, fan whirring, stool chirping, light buzzing? Finally
a coffee break. Joe will join me soon with his stories
of last weekend. I wish I had his life as a sales person,
out with the public, fresh air.

Will I ever get a promotion? Will I ever see beyond my grey,
brick, windowless walls? My stool screeches as I push away
from the bench. My light blinks off.
My fan comes to a rest.
A few minutes away from having a numb bum.

A Post Easter Resurrection

A friend died on his floor. Yes
literally died. Head bashed, hung
on baseboard, limp,
a greying-white ghost. Yes
literally, collapsed, widow mourning
his loss in hysteria, no pulse,
no verbose emanations
or tolerated, garrulous expositions passed
his blue lips, though he is still alive,
resurrected, driver's license reinstated,
but yes it is true, he did die.
You can ask him.

Now my friend, the witness to death,
is brought back to life,
faulty instrumentation forced him
to cut out junk food,
at least for a few days.
The doc says – healthy as a horse,
fit as a fiddle – relieved.

His dog is doing much better too
after a visit to the vet. The vet's bill
almost killed him, my friend that is,
not the dog.

How precarious an existence
do we ramble in our zigzagie
perilous journey from, I won or lost at cards,
to waiting for another rejection slip.
I will help him rebuild his front steps,
for him, for my mother, for our long
good byes after a yawning soak
in the hot tub and longing gaze
waiting for migrating birds to arrive
as we sit and wait for our resurrection.

Kevin Desbiens*

I used to call him Monkey Man.
His grandkids called him Popeye.
His dear wife Karey called him Bud
but no one ever dared call him:
late For Dinner.

I only knew him for a short time,
for months in fact.
Most of that time was with a bird's eye view
of a little tree-lined inlet, part of Brighton Bay
on Lake Ontario in Presqu'ile Provincial Park
where Kevin, Stan and I built a roof for Samey.
Kevin buzzed to the job site on his spiffy scooter,
often with his eye-goggled, red-scarfed
best friend, four legged Pablo, not really a dog
perched in the trailer with tools.
Kevin would brag like a proud father of the tricks
he taught Pablo – *fetch me the 2X4,*
he would say over and over, waving his arms.
Eventually Pablo would scamper off returning
tail wagging with a 2X4 clenched in his teeth.

Kevin was a nimble, sure-footed man who danced
like a monkey from rafter to rafter.
He would rather swing from the lintel to the ground
than trust an aluminum ladder.
He teased me, poked and prodded me.
He was a scalawag scooping screws from my pouch
while I had my hands full. He pulled my toque
over my eyes as I passed by.
He was an imp in the best possible way.

On our last day of work, the last nail was pounded,
the last rafter true, our job was done,
we had our picture taken. Kevin scampered
to the soffit's edge and hung down into the picture,
Monkey Man's last hurrah. At least I have the picture
on FaceBook to remember what a rascal he was.
We will miss you, Kevin The Good*.

*The last name Desbiens translates as "the good"

Roasting his Head

Manuel bent over
head inches from
the orange glowing coils
of a hot plate cooker
rotating from one ear
to the other, back and forth,
back and forth
like a roasting pig on a stick.

What are you doing my brother?
You look like you are cooking
your head. He laughs,
I am drying my hair.
We used to have
a hair blower machine,
pointing to Adonay,
but my wife gave it away.

Swollen Bellies

In the brow-beading heat of the early afternoon,
mucho mucho sol, a Cuban friend says,
climbing 150 stairs to the top of Gibara, above
the pre-revolutionary fort to the restaurant,
good prices but sometimes dry chicken,
always plenty of rice, we came across
the nonchalant scene of a mother goat licking
her twins, black and white, newborns
that had just slipped from her swollen belly
onto the grass covered hill. Looking to the red roofs
of Gibara, the ocean beyond, she is unfettered
by her putative, natural experience.

A young woman, sixteen, *pregnant*,
says our friend, on her way down the hill
She is on her way to the hospital for an abortion.
Why make a commitment to life
when you can make an appointment for termination?
After all sex is only a national sport all over the world,
second to football, soccer as we would call it.

Mother goat stops grooming her twins for grazing.
Milk to be made, an obligation
to the demands of nature.

What's this Business about the Burkinis?

Frank waved a fly from the rim of his coffee cup. *At least when the coffee is hot the damn flies don't try to sneak in for a drink and then drown. I think that the heat keeps them away but they still land on the rim of your cup with their dirty feet. I can't stand it.*

Mark laughed and swatted at his own cup, *it's not their dirty feet that I am worried about, it is their fly poop that bothers me.*

Frank pushed his cup away, *Thanks man. I wish they would bug off. I guess that is the price we pay for sitting at an outdoor patio.*

Frank placed a coaster over his cup: *Have you seen the news lately about this "burkini" business?*

Frank put air quotes around the word burkini.

It's crazy. Our society has gone nuts. They are trying to outlaw them in some parts of France. They are trying to ban women from wearing them on the beach. The issue is making its way all the way to the French Supreme Court. Bloody well had better get stopped there. No one should have the right to tell a woman that she has to go virtually naked in public if she doesn't want to. Dorothy and I were in Turkey last week and saw what looked like a Muslim family on the beach with us.

What do you mean you were in Turkey last week? You say that pretty casually. When did you go? How long were you there for? Didn't we have coffee last Saturday or was it the week before?

Frank feigned a scowl. *"It was almost three weeks ago that we had coffee at The Red Skipper'. I had to go to the Istanbul head office to make a presentation about our new project, so Dorothy came with me. We had a great four days. We were buzzed out on Turkish coffee by the time we got home. Anyway, we were on a beach one afternoon and saw this Muslim family and the wife had one of these new designer burkinis that we have been hearing about on the news. It was so foreign looking that it looked like something out of a science fiction movie. It was this gorgeous metallic aqua colour with white beaded work all over the front of the top. It had a hood that was pulled up over* her hair so that other men couldn't see the wife's hair. Every square inch of her was covered except for her hands, feet and face. The irony is that everyone was gawking at her. The double irony is that you could see the outline of her nipples through the fabric. I personally think that they look hideously uncomfortable, but I can't believe that anyone would try to outlaw them. What's this world coming to? She was all covered up from head to toe, but you should have seen him. He had a belly of ample girth that hung down over his skimpy bright red speedo bathing suit. From the front, you could hardly see he had anything on. This was not a sight that you wanted to see. They had three kids that were all frolicking in the water, all with normal swim suits on. I wonder what age they will make the nine-year-old girl start wearing a burkini, like her mom? Can you imagine all of a sudden having to wear a sweat suit with a hoodie when you go swimming?

Mark perked up and put down his coffee. In a bit of a raised voice he blurted: *You're a nut-bar man. What people are outraged about isn't that the woman's body is all covered up. They are outraged that it represents a poisonous ideology of repression against women. Some people, and I'm one of them, think that women have the right to wear whatever they want on the beach and even go topless if they want, I wish they would, and yah you are right, what about the little girl of that family? Do you think it is right that some man will one day force her to abandon her pretty bikini and abandon the bliss of the sun and waves on her skin? Do you think that it is right that she will have to give up that freedom? The brothers will be allowed to grow bellies and man boobs and go virtually naked, just like their dad but no, not the little girl.*

Frank furrows his brow: *You can say what you want but at least until the Muslim society changes and gets to be more progressive, the burkini is a good solution. At least they can go to the beach and swim. Can you imagine swimming in one of those full black body bag burkas.*

Yah, Mark sputters, *you nut-bar that's the point. How would you like to be a woman and have to wear one of those garbs, a big black tent and have to totally cover yourself when in public? You might as well put a leash on her and control her every move.*

Frank shuffles in his chair. *Don't call me a nut-bar, you nut-bar. There is a sign at the entrance to our park that says 'All dogs, large and small, must be kept on a leash.' The dog is a dog not a woman and no one wants to put a leash on a woman.*

They might as well be a dog. Roll over Rover and play dead and while you are at it, wear this burka.

Frank stiffens up. *Let's not get too far off track here. We are talking about the right to wear a burkini on a public beach. We are not going to find a solution to all Muslim women's rights in this one conversation.*

You are right, said Mark as he sat back in his chair and took a bite of his organic banana bread. *But let me say this one last thing. What appalls me is the way that Western women all around the world protested outside their French embassies waving signs confusing the issue. Any intelligent person knows that France's objection is not to the burkini, and its cousin the ugly burka body bag, but the protest is a statement to the love of women, and is not hatred for Muslims.*

Yah ok I got it, said Frank, *but it is absolutely offensive, now in the year 2016, when police with guns start policing what women should or shouldn't wear on a public beach. That should be the issue that we all rally against, not that a woman is not showing enough skin. Whether or not a segment of the population belongs to a repressive, misogynistic culture which denies females power over their own bodies is a different battle.*

Mark laughs, *Ok, one final, final word and then we can talk about the weather if you like. You said we are living in 2016, but the issue is that the Islamists aren't actually living in the 21st century. Some would say that they have not even made it into the 20th century. The Victorian era was more progressive than Muslim orthodoxy is today. Even in Victorian times, girls were more than just breeding stock.*

So we survived a summer of drought. Thank God we ended the summer with a few days of rain. Even though it has been a hot dry summer, the Farmer's Almanac says it is going to be a cold winter full of snow. Last year, we had hardly any snow. By the way, did you ever borrow a trap and relocate your family of raccoons?

Frank flipped the coaster off of his cup and sipped the last of his coffee.

Leonard Cohen and Donald Trump in the Same Sentence?

Mark and Frank sit in their favorite café for their weekly Saturday, ritual coffee. Frank flails his newspaper in the air in front shooing flies as he complains about the high price of gas. *For Pete's sake, I paid $2.26 a gallon yesterday and today the price at the pumps is up almost twenty cents, just overnight for Pete's sake. Why do we have to pay more for our gas than the rest of the country? The paper says our USA national average is $2.10 a gallon. It's just not fair. The price for everything is going up every time you turn around and they blame it all on the price of transportation. High gas prices means more expensive everything.*

As Mark goes to sit down, he grabs at Frank's paper that is still swirling in the air. *I just placed an order for our coffees. Sarah will bring them over when they're ready. Frank, you think that the price of gas is high now, you should wait until Trump is sworn in and starts messing with the economy, then, you will see high gas prices. I was reading a blog this morning that was comparing Trump with Hitler and that fuel prices skyrocketed when Hitler took power and then the German economy tanked. Oh man, don't get me started.*

Mark was already well into a diatribe that he wanted to avoid. Mark grabs at Frank's newspaper again and misses. *Frank, I'm not sure I am going to survive this current news cycle. It seems to me it's so full of shit. Trump the devil incarnate elected president of the free world, versus the old man iconic of the music world, Cohen, the saint of Pop and Rock dies at 82. They are battling it out for attention in the media. I am already tired of hearing, 'So Long Marianne' and I sure am tired of hearing what a misogynistic prick Trump is. Cohen was just as much of a womanizer as Trump, but you don't hear the media harping on that. You wouldn't want to tarnish Saint Cohen's reputation now that he's dead. I bet the sales of Cohen's newest album, 'You wanted it Darker' are going through the roof. Why does everyone want a piece of a dead guy? In Canada, they worship him as a cultural icon, even though they know in his early days, he was as much of a misogynistic prick as Trump.*

Frank swished his paper at Mark and remarked, *"It sounds like you have quite a big bee in your bonnet. Which side of the bed did you wake up on?*

Mark interrupted Frank with a quick reply. *Let me tell you what side of the bed I woke up on. I woke up on the, give Trump a chance, side of the bed. I know that Trump is probably a total misogynistic, redneck, S.O.B. It's the way the media paints him out to be, but surly he isn't all bad. Don't get me wrong, I didn't vote for him, but I also didn't vote for Hilary Clinton either. The entire country acts as if there are only two viable candidates running for president. I voted Libertarian again. Not because I thought that there was a chance in hell that Gary Johnson would be president, but because we need an alternate voice shouting from the damn rafters to make sure the government doesn't run rough shot over the people. Fabulous, thank God our coffees are coming.*

Frank shakes his newspaper at Mark. *Oh man, Mark, you don't have a bee in your bonnet, but you have a bee up your butt. You are starting to sound like Trump spouting half-truths that don't make any sense. First of all, I don't know Cohen's sexual proclivities or his past and neither do you, but even if he was a womanizer, it doesn't mean that he was a misogynistic blow hard like Trump. You can tell that Trump is a woman hater just by how he talks about women in public. Cohen's poems were not at all about disrespect of women. You are just trying to paint them both with the same broad brush you have painted yourself with.*

Frank slowly leans forward. In a low harsh voice he reminds Mark about his not so distant past and his non-existent relationship with his oldest daughter, Rachel.

I hate to bring it up again Mark but you can't compare Cohen's womanizing past with Trump, without looking in the mirror first.

Frank leans even closer to Mark. In a half whisper, he says: *You can't do what you have done in your life and not have been, and I think you still are, a misogynistic prick. No doubt you have some good qualities and that is why I still hang around with you, I think you are redeemable. You are a good person in many ways, but you still objectify women and you still haven't publicly apologized for your past deeds. Until you do, you should keep your Trump and Cohen judgments to yourself.*

Every time you talk about Trump and Cohen and call them "Misogynistic" I can't help but think about you bragging to me about you fucking this one or that one in your van, and how many different sets of footprints you have on your van ceiling. At least Cohen went into a monastery and became a monk for years. I bet he became a better person. You can bet there was a lot of reformation going on there. Maybe you should follow his example. Maybe you and Trump should join a monastery together.

Mark laughed: *Don't worry. I am sure that they would not let me inside a monastery. Leonard Cohen no doubt bought his way into the monastery and Trump probably owned it. You might get me into a monastery if I was on a trip to China and it was a tourist destination. Other than that, flake off Mr. High and Mighty.*

About the Author

Born in 1953 in Hamilton Ontario, Richard Marvin Grove runs his own publishing house, Hidden Brook Press. He is a writer, poet, editor and photographer. Better known to all his friends as Tai, he is president of the Canada Cuba Literary Alliance, president of the Brighton Arts Council and founder of the Canadian Poet Registry. Past president of the Canadian Poetry Association, he is a freelance writer and photographer who has published widely including six books, over 30 anthologies and hundreds of poems and articles in periodicals worldwide. Email: writers@hiddenbrookpress.com

Adonay Pérez Luengo

Funeral
(To my Mother)

When they carried you in a gray and almost
broken coffin to the provisory place,
your face the same, pink
like when you are asleep.
We, kept vigil over your eternal dream.
But you were unaware of the gloomy
surroundings of the funeral house
of which we never thought about:
death was never on our mind
and we evaded the subject at our table.

Shelter
(To Pablo Manuel, my little baby)

When this world of subordination
and dependence
is debased more than it usually is,
you appear like the elf in one of your fairy-tales:
now it is you, lulling me in your arms.

Nicaro

In a distant corner where memories linger,
beaches remained forgotten and broken;
sad rusty swings, sway on the breeze.
The sea seems to have lost its memory;
the crowds no longer splash playfully
in its waters, they do not even see it.
Buildings now steal the show
from the houses full of dreams.
Far away Crystal Peak, majestic, eternal,
like the world that you painted for me,
the only salvation in the distance.

About the Author

Adonay Pérez Luengo is a Professor at the University of Holguín, Cuba. She has a bachelor's degree in geography and a master's degree in Sciences of Education. A very active member of the Canada Cuba Literary Alliance, she is also the reviewer of the Spanish texts, published by Hidden Brook Press and SandCrab Books.

Shane Joseph

Looking Beyond

The ocean waters are calm when seen from the battlements of the fort above the harbour at Santiago de Cuba. To the right, Jamaica lolls in the sun, to the left, Haiti struggles amidst its destruction. Down below, in 1898, the Spanish galleons had come in single file, like innocent sheep, to be sunk by American warships lying in-wait outside the harbour. This fort is a vantage point on history, overlooking the beauty and horror of life. *Look beyond,* my wise teacher had advised, "and you will find opportunities never seen before."

There were many such moments that I captured in words while touring Cuba recently, reminding me of what life was like when I was growing up in a beautiful but impoverished tropical island, Ceylon, where the developed world was an unreachable destination. I remember climbing the Jam tree in the front yard of our family home and looking out over the paddy fields, watching the planes fly and wondering when it would be my turn to fly away.

Over the years, by a combination of looking beyond, being dissatisfied with the *status quo*, striving, and luck, I seemed to have swapped places with those fat-cat tourists who used to come to my island home. In Cuba, it was my turn to dish out the pesos, while the locals looked on hungrily. I wanted to tell them not to be fooled, that money had limits; that even in rich countries like Canada, bounty came from hard work, and that jobs could end with a slip of the stock market. But what did they know about stock markets? All they knew was that they worked hard too, so we must have some *other* unknown secret. It's because of freedom and private enterprise, I wanted to say, but being a follower of the Middle Way, I did not want to be a poster boy for Capitalism.

I returned from my trip frustrated. In retrospect, I should have told them to go to a Fort-like place and look beyond, to the sunshine and destruction in lands beyond, look at the world with all its possibilities and pick a spot to play beyond one's comfort zone. I should have told them that it was only in Cuba, these many years later, that I had realized the wisdom of my teacher's words.

The Adventures of a Wannabe Writer

Jack had always wanted to be a writer. When his buddies – many laid off in the recession—took time out to write their novels, Jack followed suit. Besides, his back was hurting from golf and he needed a sedentary pursuit.

First, he needed a writing credential, an MFA or something. He enrolled in a three-week writers' retreat where he got drunk, swapped stories and slept with some of the alumni (including a loose faculty member who came out just to get laid) and received a diploma at the end for his efforts. He learned three principles: (1) write daily, (2) write great one-page query letters until you find an agent, and (c) market yourself.

Jack followed the formula. He wrote three pages daily, mostly junk, and trashed them at night. He developed 100 versions of a query letter and sent out three queries a day, flogging the novel yet-to-be-written, because his three-pages-a-day was ending in the bin. He built a website, posted his un-trashed writing on it, blogged and twittered. He shot a movie of himself typing, and posted it on You Tube, where he got lots of hits because it was a movie about 'nothing'. He went to writers' conferences where he took workshops that repeated: *Lock yourself in a room and write because writing is a noble occupation; family and friends are distractions.* He complied until his wife left him; she had graduated from a golf widow to a writer's widow.

When his novel was complete – 1050 pages – he searched for an editor to make sense out of it. The highly-paid editor, who made a living off Jack-types, whittled the novel down to 45 pages and declared, it was only fit to be entered into a novella contest.

Jack entered novella contests, sending out 100 submissions over six months. He won nothing.

He met other hapless scribes at the conferences but he continued to attend hoping to snag that elusive agent who would recognize his spark. Since no sparks ignited, he suggested to his colleagues that they publish an anthology under a no-name publisher set up for that purpose – who'd know the difference? They did, and the 25 writers in the anthology, each bought 200 copies to sell, gift or force upon their friends. The book was ranked a bestseller in Canada.

Jack had realized his goal. He changed his handle to *writing instructor*, specializing in query letters, and started teaching other wannabes. Last heard, he has written nothing since the solitary novella, but is making lots of money. Do you know this guy?

About the Author

Shane Joseph is the author of four novels and three collections of short stories, and was the winner of the best fantasy novel award at Write Canada in 2010 for his work After the Flood. His immigrant story collection, Paradise Revisited, was short listed fort the ReLit Award in 2014. His latest collection of stories, Crossing Limbo, were released in 2017. For details visit: www.shanejoseph.com

Stella Mazur Preda

Legacy in Gold
(An exhibit of Scythian gold at the ROM:
February 18 – May 6, 2001)

Before Christ
beyond Civilizations
rooted in the Altai Mountains of Mongolia
across the steppes of ancient Ukraine
a proud enigmatic warrior culture
revelled in conquests.

Scythian burial mounds
bridges transcending the centuries
raped by archaeological grave-diggers
spirits of desecrated warriors
bare their treasures of gold.

Thundering hooves
battle cries of Scythian marauders
the heartbeat of antiquated nomads
reflect in brilliantly polished golden relics

echo in every word
imprinted on silent museum walls

Previously published in Earth Songs – A Canadian
Anthology of Verse, spring 2002,
The Ontario Poetry Society

The Garden

white daisies sprinkled among tall grasses
dot the meadow like snowflakes
on the first winter's day
black-eyed Susans
hide their secret from the world
naked boulders protrude like
gently rounded bellies of pregnant women
soon to give birth
to the mysteries of the untended garden
the setting sun splashes the darkening sky
hues of red, pink, yellow, mauve
cast a festive glow
over the unravelling spectacle
barely audible to the human ear
a soft murmur ripples through the grasses
under the brilliance of the moonlight
a supernatural world slowly unveils ...
elves and gnomes dance
a celebration of life atop the array of boulders
accompanied by a musical
incantation of fairy wings, crickets and cicadas
the ebony night has unmasked its magic.

*Previously published in Earth Songs – A Canadian
Anthology of Verse, spring 2002,
The Ontario Poetry Society*

Twister

zigs
and zags
erratically
through sycamores pines maples
skips over
shrubs crouched in hiding
indiscriminately sucks up forest giants
exposing   black lesions
leaving the wounded earth with gaping sores

soil-encrusted tentacles tremble painfully
 subterranean inhabitants hurriedly scramble
over each other
seeking anonymity
as if caught in compromising acts
the spinning grayness swerves
and accelerates
taking a short cut
tunnels through the Eldridge farmhouse
spits out
remnants of human existence
like an old man chewing tobacco
cattle juggled skilfully in mid-air
dumped randomly
bloated mounds littering
the path of promiscuous rape

dust clouds, pine trees and death
a rancid perfume blending
with the sweet smell
of newly mown
Kentucky
bluegrass

Previously published in Butterfly Dreams, 2003
by Serengeti Press, Canada, 2003

The Little Store on St. John's Road

The open door yawned its sleepy welcome
a labyrinth of aisles awaited discovery
the exploration of childhood fantasies.
Like a favourite amusement centre, it wrapped us
in good times and laughter.

In the dark of night two huge storefront windows
eyed passers-by surreptitiously.
Reflections winked in the glow of moonlight
as if guiding the approach of alien beings.

In the bliss of daylight gleaming windows winked
kaleidoscope colours of uniformly arranged candy boxes,
beckoned neighbourhood children
through the yawning door.

Thirty years later memories steered me
to the ghosts left behind on St. John's Road.
The little store had found new life as a house.
The echoing laughter of childhood ghosts
retreated to the past as I pulled away.

About the Author

Stella Mazur Preda has been published in numerous Canadian anthologies and some US, most notably the purchase of her poem My Mother's Kitchen by Penguin Books, NY. She has released two previous books, Butterfly Dreams and The Fourth Dimension and is currently working on her third book, Tapestry, to be released in 2018. Email: star.preda@cogeco.ca

Donna Allard

in my wild place

I see fields of wild flowers
afore distance dunes where shifting sands
unveil skeletal memories of dry kelp, snaking
driftwood, and summer dreams made of clouds

in stained glass pools of memory I peer through
Alice's mirror, stumbling I become a sun illusion
a daisy in a tall grass something you'd pick
and wear in your hair

this wild place tingles between its tides,
you place the daisy there, as you once
placed your lips.

Hemingway
(Senryu)

unworried conversation
downright dreamy
with the ice crackling

in defence of heron
(Dedicated to Acadian playwright Robert Blanchard)

I just noticed, window high,
the silhouette of a great blue heron
near a small lagoon that is now a
desolate surface of white moon.

Back, apparently shunned by the
lagoon's denied absence,
watches the dark forest defoliating away;
before its eyes, take refuge in the winds
shattering the mirror underfoot:
the shards of glass gut the fish below
the great red reflection is undeniable
against the pure snow.

both sides of the tweed

*(inspired by singer songwriter Laura Smith
& her visit to Scotland)*

sun cloud wings
barren tree limbs
across a trestle

brick red chair

where you sat Saturday
before the leaving
before that last shadow's eve

upon arriving I noticed the
broken chair leg – you must
have left in fury

the scooter keys remained
upon the window ledge

cobblestones leave no footprint
I stand without direction

About the Author

Canadian poet Donna Allard is the founder of Sojourner Literary Festival and past President of the Canadian Poetry Association. Email: donnaallard@live.ca

Photograph by John Hamley

Photograph by John Hamley

Photograph by John Hamley

Photograph by John Hamley

Yanet Alejo Milian

Winter Songs
Grayish Blue
(Dedicated to Betty Anne & Douglas Sinclair)

The sound of horses, galloped
trapped in carriages
full of people.

Universe of colored
leaves whirl in the street,
a hastening man with a suitcase.

Everyone eating,
junk food,
the Sun disappeared.

This breeze brushes away
the noisy crowd
around my bench.

An inquisitive ant
tries to get into my ear,
my train is coming.

Five minutes to departure,
a cold drop of water
on my cheek.

About the Author

Born in Ciego de Avila, Cuba, Yanet Alejo Milian graduated in English and French. A translator at the University of Ciego de Avila, she wrote for its newspaper. She studied creative and poetry writing and became a Canada Cuba Literary Alliance member. Her work was published in the CCLA, The Envoy newsletter, and members' anthology, Crossing Borders. Email: milianjanet71@gmail.com

Tara Kainer

For Evelyn

Mysterious as birth
your labouring and deep retreat
while outside the world lies
imprisoned in gleaming crystal,
giant spruce in the courtyard capped
with ice leaning left
comically.

Your restlessness stilled
by vials of narcotics –
we won't let her suffer
the nurses say – still
your hand, skin
thinned and stretched, taut
over jutting bones, clasps
and unclasps the bed rail.

I held your hand at first
until your blue eyes,
half-opened, clouded over
like the overcast sky:
you pulled away, I stared
while you slept uncertain
what to do, feeling voyeuristic
on discovering your intimacy
with this strange and foreign
land. *So this is Death*, I think,
this shrinking and shrinking
between these four white walls,
this hospital bed, your body swaddled
in white tangled sheets
soon to become
your funeral shroud.

Lost

Vantage point lost
for constellations, comets, falling stars,
planetary configurations, super moons
crammed between houses, confined
by fences, looming street lamps,
towering power poles,
no longer elevated
above clutter of rooftops, web
of wires, can't see night sky,
meet land clear across the water.

Cosmos blotted out by civilization
dreams of lying in sandy reeds,
lake's edge staring
into star-studded midnight
sun and moon emerging
from opposite ends
of the horizon, swirling
pinwheels of tumultuous
light, exquisite tension
between them, dissolving
as they meet
into perfectly
balanced enlightenment.

Awakened aching
for that part of me
redolent
of birthing stars,
that distant past
beyond imagining.

A mind is a terrible thing to waste
(1972 Slogan of the United Negro College Fund)

Squandered human potential
Belongs to the world's 7 million children who die
Each and every year before reaching the age of 5.
Illiteracy rates among global youth at 95% and higher.
The 65 million girls who can't go to school:

Remain at home instead as housekeepers and nursemaids
To their fathers and brothers;
Never developing the vocabulary or breadth of ideas
Capable of bridging them to higher achievements.
Human potential has something to do
With the opportunity of living into old age, like most
Average Canadians, not dying early as
Indigenous peoples and some Africans do
Decades sooner than the rest of us:

Some experts say the single best yardstick for measuring a
Person's potential is education, others income:

A disparity of 21 years exists between the lifespans of the
Richest and poorest in Hamilton, Ontario living in
Neighbourhoods barely 10 kilometers apart.

Innovation disappears when energies are devoted to the
Crushing banalities of daily existence:
You won't have much potential if you're living
A life of deprivation, chaos and confusion;

Gang and gun culture, drug and alcohol abuse are colossal,
Contributors to early death, wasters of human possibility.
Realized human potential depends on privilege, the
Luxury to pick up a paint brush, a pen,
The time to experience Nature's beauties,
Contemplate a more meaningful life.

Epiphany

On days like this
when pavement
is the colour
of the saturnine sky
and every car is a
predator, November
wind strikes
like a whip and
I'm cut to the quick
by the clerk's
derisive stare.
I can't deny
the cruelty
and contempt
of the world,
I can't shut out
this newly acquired
knowledge
my new-found
understanding
of you.

Canada 150

Canada was promise and possibility,
refuge from war
stepping off the train at Balgonie
there was nothing –
having left all behind –
but empty blue sky bending to greet
the endless horizon.
A blank canvas, she thought, upon which
it was possible to paint anything.
Winter was white on white
a trip to the barn in a blizzard
from her small sod house,
as dangerous as any expedition to Antarctica;
summer an expansion of green
steady creep of growth from
water-filled hollows to higher ground,
transforming prairie
into a matrix of colour and movement,
prairie dogs burrowing among tiny
red strawberries, wildflowers
bursting into bloom, bobolinks
and meadowlarks emblazoning the air
with song, a garden;
her grown son would recall
decades later past war and depression
secured in his suburban home, Canada,
a shining spool of progress unwinding
steadily into the future. His grandson
would inherit contracted landscape
girded by iron and steel, crisscrossing
ribbons of pavement leading even
to the top of the world: Arctic's
shrinking ice cap, melting permafrost,
poisoned water and air. Underemployed
and mired in debt, wedged

in his drab, urban apartment, divested
of hope and aspiration, a prospect
his great-grandmother, outside in her vegetable garden,
jolted to her feet by earth's sudden shaking, escalating
thunder of a million buffalo hooves, dark
shifting mass shrouded in dust, disappearing
over the horizon, wave upon wave,
could not possibly imagine …

About the Author

Tara Kainer grew up in Knoxville, Tennessee and Regina, Saskatchewan. She attended the University of Regina and Queen's University, Kingston. In 2011, Hidden Brook Press published a book of her poems, When I Think on Your Lives. The mother of three grown sons, she currently works in the social justice office of the Sisters of Providence of St. Vincent de Paul in Kingston, Ontario. Email: tara.kainer@providence.ca

Gary Rasberry

Typewriter Love

Tell me more about
Typewriter love.

How your fingers find the keys
In the dark.

Line after line
Come through. How?

The carriage return, signals the end
Of a beautiful composition, the beginning

Of another. How the fonts bleed
Ever so lightly on to the page

As you strike the keys: A memo.
A love letter. A poem. A Tattoo

How the absence of spellcheck liberates you.
Allows you to err permanently

When reckless, and oblivious. A clatter–
Of metal keys that sometimes tangle in a rush

To say everything and
More.

*Typewriter Love previously published in Some Days Just Noticing. GW Rasberry. Wintergreen Studios Press. Kingston, ON (2017)

Ready

A poem is sunrise after the darkest night;
an unexpected channeled message from the light.

Its grace extended from neglected muse,
asking to be shared, seen, heard and felt.

A poem is an inspiration
quickly written before lost,

edited, built up, carefully crafted)
until it's ready to be read.

Previously published online by Big Pond Rumours in their Winter 2015 issue, and in Part-Time Contemplative, my 2016 Lyricalmyrical chapbook.

About the Author

Juno-nominated children's artist, Gary Rasberry has been a fixture on the Kingston music and arts scene for almost three decades. A noted artist-educator, Gary has performed at schools and festivals across Ontario and beyond leaving a trail of happy children and smiling parents in his wake. Email: gwrasberry@gmail.com

Kimberley Grove

The Saint John River

It should have been romantic,
After all, it was the moon;
But all I saw was bubble-gum
A puny round peach-coloured ball
Stuck in the black throat
Of a tree-covered hill:
But maybe the moon has lost
Its significance.
Here in New Brunswick
Where the River is king
And the hills weave beside it,
Guarding and protecting
Saint John's passage to the sea;
Here the river never leaves centre stage,
While the moon lies low
Waiting, shyly in the wings,
In the shadows of greatness
Waiting for the main curtain
To be lifted
And a new day to begin.

The Eternal Refugee

Break, break
O, ancient sea,
Go ahead
Let your waves
Slash and gash
At stones in the sand;
Makes no difference
How much you stumble
And tumble over
The solid cushions
That have broken
From earth's shore;
You cannot venture
Over valley and hill,
You are a refugee
For evermore.

Cuba

Are we fooled
by the smiles,
by the taxi driver's
distaste for imperialism
by the small child's
cheerful eyes?
Are we fooled?

Are we fooled
by the easy life
of sitting by the ocean
and taking tourists sailing,
or the woman that
laughs as she teaches
aerobics in the water?
Are we fooled?

Are we fooled
when we think that
Cuba provides the good life
a life full of music and dancing
and infinite fountains of *pinacoladas*?
Are we fooled?

Are we fooled
when we see the singer's
eyes sparkle with delight
and the guitarist tease
a cranky tourist?
Are we fooled?

Do we see what we
want to see?
Is it really a prison
with no open doors
or a paradise
where you wonder
why anyone would leave?

Something Special

There is something special
About differences:
People are different
Depending from which country
They are from
Not just the customs
They have
Not just what their
Tastes are.

People can be different
In their backgrounds:
Who taught them about life
Who taught them how to care
Who instructed them
How to tie their shoes
Or bake pies, be polite.

No one is exactly the same,
Not even twins.

What makes our experiences
So special is that they are different
And we react to them differently
From other people, whether
It's family, friends, neighbours
Or strangers on the street:

They are different which makes
Them something special.

The Mist

The mist hovers over the lake
Weighing heavier with its thickness
Leaving behind an offering,
A comforting quilt of smoke
Over past agonies, past wounds, past scars,
Seeping into the harsh lines
Scraping out the
Cruel childhood memories,
Left in rocks at
The altar of Lake Memphremagog.

About the Author

Kimberley Elizabeth Grove has been published in the Globe and Mail, The Christian Science Monitor, The Toronto Star and various smaller publications. She has taught writing at Loyalist College, the Trenton Air Force Base, the Colborne Community Care Centre and Ciego de Avila University in Cuba. Her teaching comes from a love of reading what others have to share. Email: kesgrove@gmail.com

Photograph by John Hamley

Photograph by John Hamley

Photograph by Richard M. Grove

Photograph by Richard M. Grove

Ernesto Galbán Peramo

Memories

I watch old pictures casually,
trying to organize my mind.
Times gone by haunt me
with flashes of youth, love, past glories.
Promises have been left behind,
there are vague images, and I forgot
the girl in blue, vanished in bygone days.
Dry pressed flowers
in a book, broken words,
a pink handkerchief and a letter
pledging endless love.
Memories still vibrate in my mind
after so many summers.
So much has changed. Time flies!

To say Never

Never say *never;* it's quite a risk
better not plan for the future,
not before you are fully aware
our fate is also a part of our world.
To say *never* prevents the possibility
of making the right decisions:
there is human determination,
divine intervention,
the unknown; be it good or evil.
To say *never* makes us overlook
those small details, life's perspective
or will lead us to bid farewell forever.
In this world to say *never* is illogic
for our dreams can come true …
if they fade, then it is God's will.

Guilt

Guilt attacks our conscience
sneaks inside our minds
in disguise, floods our brain.
It baffles us time and again.
Guilt wears a face, spawns a shadow
when years go by;
grows huge with time turns us suicidal.
And there is no way to eliminate it.
Guilt brings oblivion controls
and harms us with its continuous persistence,
pokes into our sins revives them
whether we committed them
with intent or not. It creates insecurity,
prowls round us like a stalker
in dark places full of names and faces.

Unpredictable

The tree they planted has grown
more branches through the winters,
there will be tough and tender moments for them.
Even if the tree stays in bloom,
in spring it will have what's left
of either joy or sadness.
Like us the tree will endure and last
like us it can also wither.
Life and death come as one entity
they can happen within seconds,
then stroll down the path, hand in hand:
multi-faceted, both unpredictable,
unfazed, to all the hours
we attempt to conquer, to gain ... in vain ...

Mother

A woman I love is aging
but I have never written her a song;
for her it is natural to endure the pain
in her chest, she so often complains about.
She plaits, her grey hair: every single night
rewinds in her mind her entire life;
and when she forgets, she invites me
to help her find her missing brooch.
Time forsakes her, yet she regales me
with her incredible tender charm. She graces
the things she touches. She is my mother
and it is hard for me to put into words
what I will feel when, one of these days,
she departs to meet with my father.

About the Author

Ernesto Galbán Peramo. Professor in the University of Holguín, Cuba. He graduated with a Master's degree in History of Arts from the University of Santiago de Cuba. He is the recipient of several poetry awards and is currently involved in active radio promotion of themes about art. He works at the University's On-campus and Community Activities Department.

Danielle Dinally (known to many as DD)

A Chocolate Flavour

Let the Georgian Era paint a picture:
a key spectacle at court.
Finger picking pods of cocoa.
Fermented and fried,
fire-roasted, suave,
a dark sap that liquefies,
so satisfying to watch.
In modern days
it's said: *shaken not stirred.*

They would say: *drank not eaten.*
A show of kingship, status, power.
Beside the roast beef and plum pudding
      chocolate mixed with warm milk to help coax,
or within a port-wine – hot and
invigorating – making one lustful
in the thick of dice, dance, share stories and
scandal!
Close your eyes
inhale the aroma
as it is whisked nice and frothy.
Then try it,
the creamy and acidic aftertaste
      may never leave you.

A Convicted Boy

Ask Joan Plowright, she'll tell you:
you have to look at images differently from the
way you look at other things, more closely, see what they mean to you.
He is a teenager, but when I look, I see a child.
There's something about his eyes and face that seem lost and sad.
The skull tattoo plastered on the nape of his neck…it's not him.
Does he even know it's there?
What's his story?
A walking Oxymoron.
He made the killing, yet he rocks back and forth
frightened and confused,
so helpless behind thick glass —
I can't reach out to him.
What's his story?
What happened to him?
Why isn't there a change in his sadness?
What does he want to say that he can't?

The Beloved Keys of Cuba
(Mis Keys Queridos de Cuba),

If only I could reach through the heartbreaking pictures and embrace you. If only the salty tears that dripped from my eyes could blend with the saltiness of your oceans, to brush away the debris that fills them. Us dedicated and loyal friends from the exterior, doing what we could to help protect you, while we struggled to keep ourselves sane. Keep ourselves sane through the panic, worry, and speculation. I didn't want to tell my friends – your dancers, your customer service reps, your bartenders, all those poor souls back in Ciego and Moron, that their second home and livelihood had been *destruido** or had *desaparecido** . But I knew they were on edge, depending on us, as they awaited their fates.

I lit a candle, a virtual candle, the night before Irma struck to show that you'd be in my prayers. I was afraid to go to sleep. What if I went to sleep and something happened to you and the dwellers inside you? I tried to keep positive, but at the same time, I knew I had to prepare for the worst. I was scared. But when my eyes did open the next morning, I wasted no time. I hustled to purchase some minutes to start making my phone calls. As many as I could make in the limited time span that I had. My throat clogged, and my heart broke into three as I spoke to some friends. All of them sounded so helpless in their own way. I didn't know how to respond. What could one do in my position? Words of support? But I was at a loss of those words.

I've had a few setbacks and rough patches happening in my life a little before and around the same time. But the situations could not be compared. For the saying, "count your blessings, there's always someone in a worse situation," had come to mind. Irma stretched her black clouds over you and circled in and around you for 72 hours, turning you over good and proper. She crumbled your towns, flooded your streets, left your homes roofless, cut your power, and left your people in tears. What nature can do. What was only a short time ago, a picturesque dream, had turned into a war-zone area.

It is indeed a time of despair, however, we all know it's not the end of you. So now, as *I* personify you, I leave you to take in and mull over these wise words your inhabitants have said to me: *todos los problemas empiezan de la raiz* *, *Dios sabe lo que hace* *, and *no te vuelvas a miel* *. Yes, as time passes I notice that a lot of my friends, in and around the Keys, in and around *you*, have a habit of talking in metaphor. And not to worry, I have confidence your towns, cities, yourself the Keys, will be replenished. The only difference, more beautiful and much stronger.

destroyed
disappeared
all problems start from the root
God knows what he's doing
don't turn into honey

About the Author

Known to many as DD, Danielle Dinally is a passionate writer, poet, editor, and proof-reader. She is the current editor of the Canada Cuba Literary Alliance newsletter, The Envoy and content translator for the Canada-based Medical News Bulletin. DD comes from an Indo-Guyanese heritage and speaks and writes Spanish fluently. Email: danielledin@hotmail.com

Jorge Luis Roblejo Pérez

Uncertain Question

I am suddenly awakened by the far away music in the street
A strident voice of a street vendour shouting:
Big brown beans and bananas!
Quickly, I put on my clothes put the coffee pot on the fire:
For one second I ask myself: *Why does time exist?*
Why is this monster always feeding on our lives?
And I could ask a thousand more questions,
I could even try to solve this mystery ...
While I inhale the aroma of fresh coffee.
I am ready to go, ready to face my day:
My twenty four hours; ready to live my time,
With loud music on the streets from bike fruit vendours,
Under our tropical sun and hot weather, punctual,
Ready to forget this unforgiving God, time;
Until the new day begins again ...

The pacific brown of your dreamy eyes:
You choose the morning perfume
To feel fresh as you rise bright and shinning
Like the burning sunrise,
But I can see you anyway as you really are:
Your white humid sun-tanned skin,
Your soft long hair, like colored palm tree butterflies,
Your smile, sweeter than cold sugar cane juice in a hot afternoon,
And your beautiful eyes:
You passed away so suddenly
But I can behold you anyway.
When ... in a blink of an eye
You looked at me for the very first time,
I found myself lost in the depths of your eyes,
Discovering an entire new world
Made of multi-flavored coffees from rainy mountains,
Floating by honey riversides in a milked sky;
Walking on misty magic streets
With my soul and my heart tinted all over,
Sailing in the pacific brown of your dreamy eyes.

Life Story

I struggle through half-heartedly,–
Mutilated by unrealized dreams and illusions,
A heart submerged in shadowed whispers,
And floods of memories within.
I have a heart that livens up eagerly
Merely on smelling your perfume,
A poor heart that does not know dawn from night,
It misses the taste of happiness,
It misses the colour of dawn,
A sad heart, of incoherent consciousness
Of timeless living,
Yearning for the dream of your presence.
With patience this heart
Sews visions of victories of accomplished dreams
Coloured by the aurora:
Its sadness does not think, nor whisper,
Only relies on its strength, its faith,
Beats stronger than the wind in the blue sky;
This heart now lives
Only on a whiff of your fragrance,
Only for your love.

About the Author

Born in Bayamo in1991, Jorge Luis Roblejo Pérez graduated as an electronics technician, and studied English. A saxophone player in the provincial music band of Bayamo city and an artist, he started writing poetry and short stories when he was a child. His work appeared in the various publications by the Canada Cuba Literary Alliance. Jorge is member of the Sea Dreamers of Gibara. Email: joyph@nauta.cu

From our Editor:
Raymond Fenech

Feeding on Time

You haunt me so often
Like the wind on a wintry night,
Or the cruel sun that burns out
Every patch of the cool shade;
And I try hard to walk away
To run, escape from all the pain
You've been inflicting for years:
Leaving me deprived of joy.
And each time I hide from you,
The agony remains, I cannot shake
The ache you bring about each day.
A ghost invisible, you silently wait,
Then you leave and take with you
Part of my life, part of my youth
Whilst I watch you turn from pink to grey
Till light is defeated by darkness again.
Each day you syphon more energy;
At each sunset, I force myself to say:
Tomorrow, there will be another day,
But then each thought for tomorrow
Is lost in the mist that blocks my way
Through the pitch black, the dream;
That turns into a wakeful nightmare.
Each corner I try to turn, I feel afraid
Not knowing what's on the other end;
But when I feel so vulnerably mortal
And everything dwells on such finality,
Deep down I know, I can rely on today,
The madness of living, knowing I must die
So I must continue to feed
On what's left of you, time.

Hereafter

If only the misery and sorrow that surround me
Were not reflected in my own eyes,
Then I would see more clearly through the haze,
The mists, clouds that fold and unfold
Before every step I take unto this long road.

If only my vision was blurred and was totally blind
Immune to humans crying tears of blood,
And somehow that magic wand, I always longed for,
Since I was a child came into my hands
So I could make things better, remove the pain forever.

If only my late loved ones could continue to speak
To communicate, to advise me, still feel their love
The comforting touch of their hands, feel their warmth;
And each time I close my eyes, I see their smile
Know for sure they're better off where they are.

If only when the sun sets, the rosy pink turns black
When my mind is devoured by memories that bring back,
The joy and grief I had: only then my parents were there
To cancel forever my fear, wipe away my tears;
To sing me a lullaby, kneel down with me to say a prayer.

If only I could go back and speak to those
I never said *I love you*, for pride or momentary anger,
And they departed and I was left to say *I'm sorry*
Without ever knowing whether I had been forgiven:
Now anguished I strive on existing, instead of living.

If only I could watch a virgin world when rains were pure
And spoke with shades that spoke right back inside my brain,
Strolled among nature's wilderness, when dew caressed my knees,
When yellow carpets in the fields swayed dancing in the winds
The sea was emerald blue like in a blissful fairy dream.

If only I could go back and be born already a man
Instead of a child, with the wisdom of a grown-up;
And knew already about life, the time that makes it tick,
So when death strikes I would not even know, or be afraid
Never miss my loved ones, and quietly sleep until I simply fade.

First Night

How I still remember you
now as you cross my path
swaying your tall elegant body
your hair in pony-tail beating a rhythm
like the last samba we danced in Brazil

how your flanks still move
and I thought all was forgotten
for even now your buoyant breasts are still
the same where I had buried my blushing face
before you mounted my inexperienced erection
and rode me into light and dark
until I was dry and sweating
and after couldn't stop wanting you

how we groaned in ecstasy and I thought
this love was surely eternally sealed
and I could not forget how
my heart refused to obliterate this memory
until I saw you flirting with another
whispering sensuously your tongue probing his ears
as you had done on our first night

how my heart missed the rhythm
and my chest ached from affliction
and to this day though I've ridden
to many a light and dark
I still remember.

The Sound of Silence

Is thrashed in the wind
In its whooshing gushes,
The freezing breeze brushes
Against my blushing face
Like a cold sharp blade
Striping it bare to the skin;
And as the crisp air zips past
My sense of hearing,
I listen to the silence,
The awesome speech
Of wispy ghosts
Still remains to haunt me,
Vagrant in this empty space.
The mind, now afloat
Focuses on the void
Where solitude turns
Into a quiet frenzy,
A speechless zephyr
A breath playing music
Rasping, in winded sighs
Of hushed shushes
A muted message,
Peaceful, reticent, inaudible,
Nature's symphony at large:
It is the sound of silence.

Broken Innocence

I don't even know how we came to be
in my bedroom – you locked the door;
I was thirteen and wanted to feel
the first shiver of excitement
that came like air into a deflated balloon;
you were twelve, and also wanted something new.
So you unbuttoned my shorts,
peeled them down,
slowly, with trembling hands.
Your veins were strained
your voice husky –
you tried to hide your eagerness
but your fast breathing gave you away.
I had only dreamt this moment.
Now you were fondling my erection.
I could only moan my consent.
In vain, I tried to hide my eruption,
then you sucked my shyness away,
until I was no longer ashamed of my nakedness.
You felt for my soul right inside me.
You kissed me asking if I loved you.
But you didn't wait for my reply.
I doubt I knew what to answer.
Perhaps later – this was the first
of many sessions still to come.
We were both eager to experiment;
we both wanted to embark into the unknown.
The door was a safety barrier
against grown-ups and religion.
When I exploded and couldn't stop,
it collapsed the walls of my prison.

We both knew what we wanted;
we both got what we had dreamed about
and ate each other to the bone.
Unconsciously we saw through life
and discovered a shade of grey.
Then, rains fell abundantly outside
and lightning tore us apart.

Broken Innocence: a) Boston Poetry Magazine,
USA, 2014; b) Blood Lines, poetry collection,
SandCrab Books, Cuba, 2012

My First Youthful Illusion of Immortality

When I was young I never really thought about death. It was like I was immune to it and thought that most people were because all those family members and friends that were in my life were all still fairly young, healthy and untouchable.

I think that this impression was also due to the fact that people then were not so well informed about the many lurking illnesses and maladies which kill so many on a daily basis. There were no daily TV adverts warning people about heart disease and the various kinds of cancer, such as lung, breast and prostate cancer which have become so common now a day. TV adverts today even advise you to take an insurance so your family will have the money to cover your funeral expenses – now isn't that a nice and cheerful thought to start the day with?

My Godfather who was a doctor and general practitioner used to say that a little knowledge is a dangerous thing. I speak for myself, I really think that living in constant fear that one might die of one of these illnesses is also bad for health. I often think that just maybe if we weren't so much aware of all these dangers then perhaps we could get on with our lives and live them to the full without the constant obsessive fear that we have cancer, or that at some point we might drop down dead.

As time passed, I realized that life is like a time bomb, the moment one is born, the clock starts ticking the days, the hours and the minutes away until that one fine day when one passes away. It's good to know that man is mortal and everyone has an expiry date, but do we really need to rub it in so much to the point that we make life seem as if every person is going to succumb to cancer or heart disease? We all have to die. What does it really matter what will kill us? In the end, wouldn't it have been better to make the most of our lives living dangerously and fearlessly enjoying every moment of it all?

The first shock of my life came when I was about 13. I was attending secondary school at St. Albert the Great College in Valletta. It was a private school run by the Dominican Fathers after being awarded a five year scholarship by the Government.

When I started attending St. Albert the Great College, I remember that half way through the first term, a boy by the name of David was admitted as a late comer. He was a very sensitive boy of a very fair complexion with fair hair to match. His only 'problem' was he was very fat and some of the boys in the classroom used to make fun of him. Throughout the first year and the second David seemed also very sensitive and used to get frequent headaches. They must have been very bad headaches because each time he got one, he used to end up crying and the teacher used to send for his mother to come and pick him up to take him home. I don't think that any of his classroom mates ever thought this was the beginning of something really serious because he continued to miss lessons but always came back at some point.

The end of the second year came with the summer holidays. It was half way through summer when one Friday night, dad received an urgent call from his boss. Dad used to work at the Passport Offices in Valletta. His boss explained to him that he had been asked to issue an urgent passport for a family of three that same evening as the persons had to leave for the UK the very next day. Dad's boss came for him only a few minutes after the call. I didn't wait up for dad and when he came back from the office, I was already asleep. The next day, I went down for breakfast and saw the brand new passport on the living room table ready to be picked up. I was curious and casually I opened it to take a look at the photos. I wasn't expecting what I saw: it was David with his parents. I asked dad what the urgency was and he told me their son David needed urgent brain surgery. This news immediately made me realize that David's tantrums at school and his frequent headaches was due to some serious illness which required surgery. I was glad that unlike some of the other school boys, I hadn't gone about calling him 'a cry-baby' but instead sympathized with him and always backed him up. However, it never occurred to me that his operation was life threatening.

Summer holidays were soon over and I was back at school on my first day to start the third year. Most of my schoolmates were all gathered in the school yard waiting for the headmaster to make his annual commencement speech. Suddenly, I realized that David was not around. I went up to Anthony, one of my other school friends who lived in the same village as David and asked him why David hadn't come to school on the first day. He looked at me with sad eyes and replied:

Don't you know what happened to David?

No, I replied, I only know, he went abroad for brain surgery.

Well, he will never be back I'm afraid.

At first I thought he had his operation and his parents decided to stay in England in case he needed further treatment.

What do you mean, he will never be back?

David is gone, he never woke up from his surgery. He passed away during the operation.

I was so shocked I had to turn away. I tried to swallow hard but I felt a huge lump in my throat and then tears started rolling down my cheeks abundantly. Anthony realized I was really distraught and took me aside and spoke softly.

Ray, be thankful he passed away because in the last weeks before the operation, he was in a terrible state. I visited him at home before he left for the UK and his parents told me that his headaches had increased because the tumour was blocking some part of his brain and the blood circulation. Even if the operation had succeeded, he would have probably lived in a vegetative state as an invalid. There was no more hope for him. Surely he is better off where he is now.

A concelebrated Mass was organized by the school teachers for David that same week at the school chapel. His distraught parents were also present and I basically cried throughout the function. I just couldn't believe my friend was gone and we never even had a chance to say goodbye. Why was life so unfair? David was such a good kind person – why did God have to pick him? Couldn't he have picked up one of the many evil people who were a total waste of space and were in this world with a mission to harm other people and to give them heaps of grief?

The shock was like a wake-up call. I think that when David passed away, I left my childhood behind me for good. It was the time when I suddenly started to fear death because it could strike all those people I loved at some point without any warning. I also realized that death did not distinguish between young and old, not apparently between good and evil.

Matchmaking Wine with Food

Over the years, several wine experts have written voluminously about wine matched with food, as if there was some sort of special chemical formula that determines that a certain type of wine must be served strictly with that certain type of food. Almost all forgot that after all, it's just a matter of taste and opinion. Having said that, there are a few pointers, which could assist to increase the chances of enjoying one's bottle of wine.

Eating heavy foods necessitate heavy wines, so if you are eating a steak, choose a *Chateauneuf-du-Pape* and a *Chablis*, or some other crispy wine with your oysters.

The next suggestion follows the same pattern as the first – if you are eating great food, at a first class restaurant, choose an uncomplicated wine. If you have chosen a simple menu, then choose a great wine. First class roasted lamb can be washed down with any good mature red wine without fussing for the greatest on the wine list.

Whatever you do when you serve a special recipe with a strongly flavoured sauce, keep this in mind and not what's cooked in the sauce, fish, meat etc. If you have used wine in the sauce, serve something similar.

All wines have a certain amount of acidity especially sweet wines. It is this same acidity that keeps a wine fresh. So, if you choose a wine that is too acidic for the food, simply add a sprinkle of vinegar or lemon juice. This method is quite an asset, as you will realise, the wine will then, be more gentle on your palate. Incidentally, rich fatty foods are marvellously counterbalanced by the wine's acidity

Try eating food that is a bit sweet like gammon cooked in Irish Whisky Sauce and then choose a wine that isn't. No doubt your taste buds will feel rather irritated by the acidity and bitterness of the wine. So, it would be recommendable to drink an all-out dessert wine, which should be at least ripe with a fruity flavour.

So many people I know will insist that a red wine is served with meat and white with fish. All this is a matter of opinion. Try the opposite for a change and go by your taste. If you feel red goes down just as well with fish, why not?

Most people finish off a sumptuous dinner with cheese. Again, some would insist on red wine, but white wine especially sweet, could prove to be just as palatable.

After dinner or lunch, I am in favour of serving a variety of cheeses, so it's best to experiment and see which wine tastes good with all the brands you intend to serve at your dinner table.

Moderate Wine Drinkers are Healthier

The first and oldest known medical handbook was produced around 2,200 BC. It was written on a clay tablet and recommended wines for various illnesses.

In recent years, there have been several news items saying that wine combats heart disease. To this effect, scientists at the *Universite de Bourgogne* have discovered that people who drink half a litre of red wine on daily basis have a higher level of High Density Lipoproteins (HDL), which keeps cholesterol away from the artery walls.

Especially the *Pinot Noir* grape contains a high concentration of Resveratrol, an anti-fungal compound which improves the lipid profile of volunteers, who drink three glasses of red wine every day for a couple of weeks. Resveratrol is actually twenty times more powerful in its antioxidant affect than Vitamin E.

For those who didn't know, both red and white wine counters both diarrhoea and constipation. White wine in particular stimulates the urinary functions. Cholera Bacteria, Typhoid and Trichinella* are killed by wine.

Dr. Heinrich Kliewe, a researcher believes that moderate amounts of wine can counteract some of the side effects caused by antibiotics.

Actually, Sir Alexander Fleming once said that *if penicillin can cure those who are ill, Spanish sherry can bring the dead back to life.*

Dr William Osler (1849-1919) stated: *The beverage alcohol is our most valuable medicinal agent – and it is the milk of old age.* Another saying about wine from **The Talmud** is that *wine nourishes, refreshes, and cheers ... wherever wine is lacking, medicines become necessary.*

Having started with a quotation from Hemingway, I feel it would be just to end in the same way quoting him again: *"Wine... offers a greater range of enjoyment and appreciation than possibly any other purely sensory thing which may be purchased.*

*Trichinella is the genus of parasitic <u>roundworms</u> of the <u>phylum</u> <u>Nematoda</u> that cause <u>trichinosis</u> (also known as trichinellosis). Members of this genus are often called trichinella or trichina worms. A characteristic of Nematoda is the one-way digestive tract, with a pseudocoelom (body cavity made up of only an ectoderm and endoderm). The genus was first recognized in a larval form in 1835. The L1 larvae live in a modified skeletal muscle cell. The adult worms occupy a membrane-bound portion of columnar epithelium, living as intramulticellular parasites. Infections with this genus have been reported from more than 150 different naturally or experimentally infected hosts. It has been shown to have a worldwide distribution in domestic and/or <u>sylvatic</u> animals. Trichinella is known as the smallest human nematode parasite, yet it is also the largest of all <u>intracellular parasites</u>. Oral ingestion of larvae–contaminated tissue is the usual route of infection, but congenital and mammary transmission can occur in rats

Good Food and Spirits of the Intoxicating Kind

I distinctly remember my great grandfather defining wine as *the water of life* and in his case it was like prophesying that he would live well over ninety years, which incidentally he did. I am told he drank at least half a litre of wine every day with his dinner.

Wine is the most civilized thing in the world, stated the Nobel Prize winning author, Ernest Hemingway and everyone knows what a terrific life Ernest had even if in the end he committed suicide. Whichever way you put it, wine has always harboured that certain magical formula which has enchanted mankind from the beginning of time.

The Satanists

It was early November when the editor of a leading newspaper called me and asked me to meet him. I had no idea what it was all about, but having worked for other leading newspapers before, I thought he wanted to assign me a piece of writing. So that same day, I went to the offices of the newspaper and met him. He went straight to the point by asking me a very strange question: *Have you been reading the newspaper lately and have you seen our reports about the satanic group that has been desecrating graves by stealing human remains from various cemeteries?*

Yes, I've been following the stories with great interest, why?

I know you are into the paranormal and that's the reason why I have called you. I have received some threatening letters from one of these groups and was wondering if you would be interested to follow the case as a freelancer?

Yes, I would love to – do you still have the letters?

Yes, here is the latest one I received.

The editor handed me a letter which contained an inverted pentagram two strange symbols and the paper was purposely burnt at certain points. The anonymous author wrote the following:

Dear Editor,

The contents of this letter are not to be printed. I am writing to you to complain about what you have published about our activities already. If you print this, Satan and all his demons will come down and burn your soul in a lake of fire where you will meet Lucifer himself face to face.

As you know already, there is black magic in Malta and evil spirits everywhere. Some of them are watching you. As you can see, I am writing this letter on this paper because it symbolizes something that you should all know. Those people who think there are no black magic rituals in Malta are wrong because there are. If you still don't believe, at some point, someday, you will be faced with the truth!

So keep your distance and do not act rashly thinking this is all some sort of silly joke. Consider this as a warning. We will persecute you, or anyone else who dares even attempt to stop our mission of reviving the true God that should be glorified in this world. WE know every move you make and we will take our revenge on you, or any of your colleagues when you least expect it. We can harm you at a distance and all sorts of accidents can befall you or your family, accidents so horrendous, gory and painful that your grief will end your life on this earth.

Beware and take heed of our warning. There will be no more in future – only an agonizing death will be the announcement to you or whoever dares follow your steps in the investigation; then you will know our promise has been kept!

Glorify Satan and pray for his protection – he is the only one capable of giving you whatever your heart may desire!

The letter was of course unsigned.

I have tried to find the meaning of the symbols on the letter but didn't manage. However, the inverted pentagram which was at the top of the letter is known to be used in witchcraft and occult rituals to conjure evil spirits.

In the meantime, I contacted a person whom I knew had recently left a satanic group which he had found himself joining without really knowing what he was in for. Of course, when the going got tough, he was shocked and miraculously managed to leave the group, or so he thought. Week after week he was having trouble with everything he usually excelled in, including at his work place and then even at home.

He knew exactly where his group used to meet and was willing to take me to see the place. He wanted to help me because he really wanted to leave the group and was prepared to go to any length if only to get rid of the ties he had with them and which he couldn't get rid of. We agreed on a date and I picked him up from home at around 5.30p.m. I had just bought a new car and though at this stage, this detail might seem irrelevant to the story, later on will turn out to be very important.

Before going to the alleged meeting place, I had also made an appointment with a leading Roman Catholic exorcist priest as I wanted to ask him a few questions. We met Fr. Clement who was very much aware of what was going on in the cemeteries and how the parts of human bones were being used in satanic rituals. Having been a reporter for quite a few years, I wasn't the gullible type of person who would believe everything people said, but this particular priest who was recommended to me as very knowledgeable person on this subject told us things that seemed to have come out of a book by Dennis Wheatley.

One of the things he said, which impressed me most and that evening took away my appetite was that satanic groups actually organized banquets, during which oven-baked human foetuses were served as a delicacy with baked potatoes. Female members of the satanic group were actually impregnated for the purpose of being able to extract the foetus before their pregnancy became obviously visible. In this way, there was no way the police could ever suspect that something illegal was going on and could not indict them for murder. Abortion in Malta is considered a murder and a heinous crime.

There were other detailed descriptions, but I had no need to write down what he told us that day because I had a pocket tape recorder. Another point he kept insisting on was that the satanic group would know the person or persons who was investigating their organization and that it was very dangerous not to be fully prepared and extra careful whilst carrying out our investigations. Before we departed, Fr. Clement gave us a special blessing to protect us from evil.

As I said, the month was November and when we left the small chapel, where we had interviewed Fr. Clement, it was already dark. We got into my car and I started the engine. I switched on the lights but there were none. I switched off the lights and turned them on again, but it seemed something was electrically wrong with my car. We were supposed to go to the place where the satanic group were meeting regularly, but the spot was off the beaten track and I wasn't going to risk driving all that way in pitch darkness. I tried to fiddle with the fuse box but to no avail. So in the end, we had no option but to postpone the meeting to another day.

However, we still had the problem of driving back home since we were quite a few miles away and I didn't fancy driving my new car in total darkness.

In the end, we decided to wave down a taxi and asked the driver if it would be alright if one of us took a lift with him and the other drove the car behind his. The taxi driver was extremely nice and we managed to get my friend home safe and sound. I drove my car all the way back home without lights.

I opened my garage and drove my car inside. Before I switched off the engine, something told me to try the lights again and behold they came on as if nothing had ever been wrong with them. I wasn't relieved in the least bit, on the contrary, I immediately remembered what Fr. Clement had told us repeatedly: *The satanic group know you are on their trail.* I felt a cold shiver going down my spine and I was genuinely frightened.

I tried to brush these thoughts away, but couldn't and for the rest of the evening I was quite uneasy. The night was long and a very loud thunder storm kept me awake all night. I wanted to get to the bottom of this mystery, so next day, the first thing I did was to take my car to an electrician. I left it there for a few hours and when I went back for it, the man told me that there was absolutely nothing wrong with it. He told me that perhaps I hadn't turned on the switch properly, but I knew I had because I had tried the switch many times the previous evening before I decided to wave down a taxi. I went home somewhat confused and have to admit that I was worried and afraid.

I had just got married and didn't want to drag my wife into something that was beyond my comprehension. My wife hated these things and anything to do with the paranormal, so I was quite certain she would be worried even more if she got to know the whole story. For the next few days, I wasn't altogether quite present at home and Angela's intuition told her something was wrong. She pressed me to tell her what had happened and finally I thought it best to share this experience with her and hoped I would feel better. Angela was horrified when I told her about the investigations and the subsequent strange events. Angela is also very super– stitious, which didn't help at all. In the end, she made me promise to drop the investigations, something which I did temporarily.

Some weeks after, something came up in the form of information about my investigations. I tried to get in touch with the person who was supposed to take me to the satanic group's meeting place, but he informed me they had changed the location. In the meantime, the desecration of graves at some of the main cemeteries had suddenly stopped. To me this was a strong indication that the police were hot on the trail of the vandals and this probably kept them quiet for a while. My contact was to phone me as soon as he discovered the new venue of their meetings, but I never heard from him again.

For those asking how come I did not record Fr. Clement's interview, which undoubtedly would have proved very interesting, please note that I did, but when I tried to rewind the tape, the gadget did not catch a single word he said. Those who are thinking that just maybe the tape recorder was damaged, I can assure you it wasn't, because I used it many times after this interview and it always worked well.

Despite the fact I am still very much interested in the paranormal, I have decided to keep my research and work strictly to ghostly apparitions, poltergeists and UFOs. I no longer explore black magic, satanic activity or evil spirits and when I inevitably do come across such cases, I always pass them on to a professional exorcist, or some other organization that is more competent to deal with such phenomenon.

The Illicit Love Letter

Despite the fact that my grandma hated my mother, she used to go regularly to her house to help her wash the floors and do the washing. Of course mum kept hoping that her mother-in law would change her mind about her and at least treat her the same way she treated the wives of my dad's two other brothers. In the end, it all turned out to be the greatest illusion in my mother's life because her mother-in law continued to do her utmost to denigrate her reputation as much as she could by inventing stories that weren't true. When dad used to visit his mother, he always returned home angry and this was because she was always picking on something so that when he returned home, he would turn on the heat on my mother.

One fine day, my mother went as usual to her mother-in law to help her with the house work. She seemed to be in a better mood than usual and my mother thought it would be polite to ask her if she had received some good news. As a matter of fact she had received a letter from an English friend who hadn't written to her for a while. The only problem was that she was illiterate and couldn't read his letter which was in English. The next thing she knew, mum was asked by grandma if she could read out the letter. My mother obligingly consented and went on to read the letter, something that she regretted doing for the rest of her life.

Dear ...

First I know I owe you an apology and I fear that this might not be enough after our accidental but providential meeting on that day when we bumped into each other and I upset your shopping bag. Since then, we never looked back and despite you are married, we knew that our love at first sight was an event neither of us could ignore.

My absence from the island was inevitable as I was called to the base with urgency by the War Office in London. There is no excuse for my neglecting you by not even writing to you with news in all these months. I am hoping you will forgive me for my stupidity when I allowed doubts to haunt my mind and forcing me to ask questions whether I was still in your heart and soul.

As my mother continued to read the letter, she started to become more uncomfortable and embarrassed as all of a sudden, she found this was a very confidential love letter and the man who wrote it would surely have never imagined my grandma would ask her daughter in-law to read it out to her. Evidently, the Englishman was an officer in the Royal Navy and must have been stationed in Malta during the war.

That's where grandma had met him. The letter continued as follows:
There isn't one single day or night that I don't think about you, about those intimate nights when we made love at your home whenever your husband was working nightshifts. In all my years, I have never experienced such sexual fulfilment and I am dying to empty my bottle inside you once again. I am really hoping that you are just as eager to meet with me and that once again, we can continue where we left off the last time.

My mother was too embarrassed to tell her mother-in law what was really in the letter, so she started doing her best to skip some of the sentences, which were of a great intimate nature and hoped that her mother in-law would not find out later what was really in the letter.

From the love letter, my mother discovered a great deal of secrets about her mother in-law. Secrets she could have never even imagined in her wildest dreams. This letter had just revealed her fiancé's mother had had a lover for several years. Apparently, he worked for the Royal Navy and visited Malta on regular basis. For some reason, he hadn't visited for some time and it looked like he was missing his mistress in Malta.

Mum wasn't sure whether to tell dad or not, but in the end she did and was surprised to discover that dad had known this all along. He knew his mother had a lover and that was probably the reason why his dad was so abusive with him. Dad's mother used to confide in her son and trusted him more than she trusted her husband. Dad's father realized this or might have even suspected something was going on but he had always been very much of a hen-pecked husband. As time went on he became terribly jealous and did everything in his power to take his revenge out on my father.

The result was devastating for dad because his music and singing career was ruined before it could really take off and his uncle's death sealed his fate. His uncle, Lorenzo who was dad's mentor, being a *Maestro di Cappella*, a composer and band master had recognized that his beloved nephew was blessed with a beautiful and unique naturally gifted tenor's voice. So, he had taken him under his wings to see to it he would become the great tenor many people expected him to become. Many had already heard him sing and at 14 he made his first debut as the *Rigoletto* at his school that had decided to stage the opera for some special anniversary occasion.

Dad's parents being both afraid of the great influence Lorenzo (dad's uncle and mentor) had with his brother who was the Archbishop of Malta, did not dare interfere. Unfortunately, he passed away suddenly in his early forties when he contracted pneumonia. That sealed my father's fate and at 14 his parents locked him up in a Capuchin convent in Gozo. In the 1930s, many parents would do anything to see their sons being ordained priests or monks, not only because it was a great honour, but priests also had financial stability for the rest of their lives and many times helped their parents by giving them money every month.

Dad hated the convent, never wanted to become a priest, never mind a monk, but he was forced to remain there until he became of age, when he finally left and walked straight into the offices of the King's Own Malta Regiment to enlist. It was 1940, just a few weeks after the news had spread that WWII was now inevitable.

About the Author

*Twice Pushcart Literary Prize nominee in 2017, Dr Raymond Fenech embarked on his writing career at 17, working as a freelancer and journalist with The Times & Sunday Times of Malta. He has published work in 13 countries and is a qualified writing, journal and poetry therapist. His research on Maltese ghosts was published in The International Directory of the Most Haunted Places, Penguin Books, USA. The Incident of the Mysterious Priest (short stories) & Growing with the Shadows (poetry collection) will be shortly launched at the international book fair, Expo America, New York.
Email: writer@go.net.mt*

List of Authors
Listed alphabetically by first name

- Adela González-Longoria Escalona – p. 133
- Adonay Pérez Luengo – p. 216
- Bob Wood – p. 25
- Bruce Kauffman – p. 48
- Chris Faiers – p. 94
- Colin Morton – p. 83
- Connie Kinnell McKinney – p. 113
- Danielle Dinally – p. 255
- Debbie Carpenter – p. 123
- Donna Allard – p. 225
- Dorothy Cox Rothwell – p. 127
- Ernesto Galbán Peramo – p. 250
- Eugenio Ernesto González Aguilera – p. 120
- Gary Rasberry – p. 239
- George Elliott Clarke – p. 103
- Graham Ducker – p. 13
- Heide Brown – p. 136
- Hugh Hazelton – p. 131
- James Cockcroft – p. 183
- James Deahl – p. 146
- Jennifer Footman – p. 75
- Joanne Culley – p. 142
- John B. Lee – p. 62
- John Hamley – p. 52
- Jorge Alberto Pérez Hernández – p. 156
- Jorge Luis Roblejo Pérez – p. 259
- K.V. Skene – p. 108
- Keith Inman – p. 169
- Kimberley Grove – p. 24
- Lisa Makarchuk – p. 194
- Manuel de Jesús Velázquez León – p. 69
- Manuel García Verdecia – p. 185
- Mary Lee Bragg – p. 199
- Miguel Ángel Olivé Iglesias – p. 29

- Miriam Estrella Vera Delgado – p. 98
- Norma West Linder – p. 174
- Raymond Fenech – p. 261
- Richard Marvin Grove (Tai) – p. 208
- Shane Joseph – p. 218
- Stella Mazur Preda – p. 13
- Sterling Haynes – p. 21
- Tara Kainer – p. 233
- Yanet Alejo Milian – p. 232

List of Photographers

Listed alphabetically by first name

John Hamley – p. 8, 9, 10, 42, 44, 46, 47, 60, 61, 88, 92, 93, 192, 228, 229, 246, 247, 248, 249

Richard M. Grove – p. 12, 89, 193, 248, 249

Shane Joseph – p. 10, 43, 190

Wency – Wenceslao Alexander Rosales – p. 11, 45, 90, 91, 191

www.ingramcontent.com/pod-product-compliance
Lightning Source LLC
Chambersburg PA
CBHW021430080526
44588CB00009B/482